Unlearn

PER
SPEC
TIVA

Introducing Perspectiva Press
Soul food for expert generalists

Perspectiva seeks to understand the relationship between systems, souls and society in a time of crisis, and to develop methods, grounded in an applied philosophy of education, to help us meet the challenges of our time.

As part of this broader endeavour, Perspectiva Press will specialise in short books with occasional longer works. These books will be well-presented and distinctive. Their purpose is to shape and share thinking that helps to:

- create a community of expert generalists with skills of synthesis and epistemic agility
- envisage a world beyond consumerism, and pathways for how we might get there
- support sociological imagination in a dynamic ecological and technological context
- cultivate spiritual sensibility; clarifying how it manifests and why it matters
- encourage a more complex and systemic understanding of the world
- commit to going beyond critique, by developing vision and method
- indicate how we can do pluralism better; epistemic, cultural, political, spiritual
- clarify what it means to become the change we want to see in the world
- develop the authority of people doing important work aligned with Perspectiva

It is unusual for a charity like Perspectiva to become a publisher, even a small one, but we value books as dignified cultural artefacts with their own kind of analogue power, and we believe ideas travel further and connect more deeply when they are rooted in the mandate of a publication designed to last for years, not merely moments. We also see a gap in the market for books that specialise in the kinds of integrative and imaginative sensibilities that speak to the challenges of our time.

Already published:

The World We Create: From god to market *Tomas Björkman*
An entrepreneur offers an historical perspective on achieving a more meaningful and sustainable world

To be published in 2021:

The Entangled Activist: Learning to recognise the master's tools *Anthea Lawson*
A seasoned campaigner on how your sense of agency changes when you realise 'getting the bastards' is not working

Collective Wisdom in the West: Beyond the shadows of the enlightenment *Liam Kavanagh*
A cognitive scientist and contemplative on the nature of 'collective wisdom' and what we need to do to get there

The Politics of Waking Up: Power and possibility in the fractal age
Indra Adnan
A psychosocial therapist on refashioning politics by meeting people where they are

Dispatches from a Time Between Worlds: Crisis and emergence in metamodernity *Authors include Jonathan Rowson (ed), Layman Pascal (ed), Zak Stein, Bonnitta Roy, Daniel Görtz, Lene Rachel Andersen, Sarah Stein Lubrano, Minna Salami, John Vervaeke and Christopher Mastropietro, Tom Murray, Mark Vernon and Jonathan Jong, Siva Thambisetty, Jeremy Johnson, Brent Cooper*
An anthology of metamodern scholars and writers on our world-historical context and pathways to cultural renaissance

Unlearn intertwines the political and the personal, the individual and society, the past and the future. It enables us to take fresh perspectives on today's existential challenges, and thus deserves many readers.

Tomas Björkman, author of The World We Create *and founder of the Ekskäret Foundation*

Worldwide we are approaching a much-needed learning revolution which calls for a better understanding of what "unlearning" is. With a simplicity "on the far side of complexity", this book offers a refreshingly clear, concise and coherent compass for navigating the transformative journey interwoven together as individuals, organizations, and societies.

Aftab Omer, President, Meridian University

What is freedom and self-determination? How do individuals and society relate to one another in the western world? Hanno Burmester wrote the book on the actual crisis of the western world without it being a Corona book and shows above all what one has to unlearn in order to advance oneself and society.

Prof. Maximilian Benz, University of Bielefeld

Unlearn integrates perspectives we have become used to dividing: the I, the We, and the World. It is a systemic book, nudging its readers towards reconsidering their position within the greater environment. It challenges us to push and expand the boundaries of everyday discourse.

Dr. Bernd Schmid, Founder, Institute for Systemic Consulting, Wiesloch

Unlearn

A Compass for
Radical Transformation

Hanno Burmester

Perspectiva Press, London, UK

systems-souls-society.com

First published in 2021

ISBN (pbk) 978-1-9998368-3-2

ISBN (ebk) 978-1-9998368-5-6

© 2021 Hanno Burmester asserts his moral right to be identified as the author of this book.

All rights reserved. No part of this publication may be reproduced, stored in a retrieval system or transmitted in any form without the prior written consent of the copyright owners, other than as permitted by UK copyright legislation or under the terms and conditions of a recognised copyright licensing scheme.

llustrations by Catharina Burmester

Cover design Studio Sutherl&

Typeset in Baskerville and Akzidenz Grotesk by www.ShakspeareEditorial.org

Printed by TJ Books Limited, Cornwall

Contents

Introduction: An era of unbecoming   1

Part I Individual Transformation

1 Core Knowledge: The future within us (sensing the new – i)   11

2 Unlearning: Letting go of who we learned to be (the patterns that hold us down – i)   26

3 Breaking Barriers: Levers towards the core self (levers towards the new – i)   37

Part II Organisational Transformation

4 The Shadows of the Past: How we limit organisations, and us in them (the patterns that hold us down – ii)   53

5 Unfolding Human Uniqueness: Towards cultures of self-authorship (sensing the new – ii)   62

6 The Seeds of Transformation: Levers for organisational unlearning (levers towards the new – ii)   76

Part III Societal Transformation

7 The Pain We Cause: Confronting the destructive society (the patterns that hold us down – iii)   91

8 From Paralysis To Transformative Purpose: Towards future society (sensing the new – iii)   108

9 Accessing the Future: Levers for transforming society (levers towards the new – iii)   118

Epilogue   135

Acknowledgements   141

Illustrations

Figure 1 Individual Transformation — 18

Figure 2 Values Tree (source: SelfLeaders/Unlearn) — 45

Figure 3 Individual Ikigai — 47

Figure 4 Organisational Transformation — 78

Figure 5 Organisational Ikigai — 80

Figure 6 Pre-Modern Model — 95

Figure 7 Today's Model — 97

Figure 8 The Model We Need — 114

Figure 9 Societal Transformation — 120

Introduction
An era of unbecoming

WESTERN SOCIETY is in deep crisis. It seems that our world is falling apart, whether you are looking from the political, social or ecological perspective. At the same time, we know that today's shifts are just the tip of the iceberg. In the coming years, the climate crisis will shake the fundament of global civilisation with rising frequency and intensity.

In the global North, a realisation is manifesting: our lifestyle, as cultivated since the early days of industrialisation, is turning out to be untenable. This lifestyle – which was never designed as a universal model, but as the privilege of a tiny, white global aristocracy – has been made possible by historically unseen levels of ecological and social exploitation. Yet this is the very lifestyle we exported globally during the second half of the 20th century, promoting an extremist ideal of economic liberty while pushing the ecosystem beyond its limits.

Even though the severity of today's situation is abundantly clear, democratic societies seem incapable of changing course. As of 2020, no democratic government has come up with any fundamental measures that mirror the seriousness of the climate crisis. Some of the symptoms of the crisis are being tackled, while its roots stay untouched. Somehow, we manage to detach knowledge from action: a widening delta that enables us to leave unaltered the paradigms and patterns we know are untenable, but which have become an integral part of what we believe constitutes a good life.

The reason for this wilful ignorance lies in the deeper nature of today's crisis. The climate crisis is a crisis of identity. It forces us to reconsider what we can rightly consider normal, and to acknowledge that the life we lead is a life based on privilege; a privilege we have grown used to over generations, thus moving it into a blind spot of our self-perception. We would have to do away with it if we were to truly change course. This, of course, would equal the undoing of our self-image: who we have learned to believe we are, and what our place is in this world.

In other words, ending the aristocratic lifestyle of capitalist exploitation is impossible without transforming our culture, which is built on principles of superiority and ecological and social exploitation. This is what makes tackling the climate crisis so difficult. The planet's reaction to our past and present actions forces us to reconsider the privileges we perceive as normal, and thus asks for a critical assessment of who we have become. We are forced to reflect on what kind of living is acceptable, and are being pushed towards fundamentally reassessing our position within the wider context of the ecosystem and global society.

It comes as no surprise, then, that for decades we opted to do nothing, even though we knew that this inaction would end in disaster. Indeed, we instead place our hope in ideas like climate engineering – technologies that are mostly non-existent, or risky and untenable. Mere hope: helping us to persist with the modern understanding of progress that is so deeply woven into our societal DNA, the belief that, as time progresses, our societies improve, driven by human idea and action.

Why do we put so much hope into creating innovations that enable us to continue with this insanity, instead of trying to become sane? What else, one wonders, must happen for us to fundamentally reconsider our position? We are, after all, at liberty to change course. The economic system is human-made, and thus can be reconfigured. So is our culture – the collective values, norms, mindsets – that serves as the fundament and driver of this system.

Our unwillingness to transform begins to make sense once we start treating the climate crisis as a crisis of collective identity. If we do so, transformation stops seeming like a purely technocratic challenge, something to be achieved by implementing the right policies. Instead, it becomes a challenge of unbecoming: of changing the deep structure of society, and of finding values and worldviews that enable us to collectively reintegrate into the ecosystem's boundaries. To be able to meet this challenge, we must acknowledge who we have become, in all its ambivalence, and identify those parts of our culture that hinder us from developing a less destructive ecological and social footprint. Only then can we cultivate a more meaningful approach to how we see ourselves in this world, and how we act within its natural boundaries.

In other words, the transformation of society is a deeply human challenge. This is why it is so important that we do not speak about societal transformation in terms of an abstract issue. Societal transformation is driven and 'made' by the transformation of individuals and groups of people. To fundamentally transform as society, the smaller parts that make and mirror the whole must transform: individuals, on the one hand, as potential initiators and drivers of societal change; and organisations, on the other, as structures that help us organise human collaboration, and create impact that goes beyond what individuals can achieve on their own.

Transformation: the case for an integrated perspective

This book makes the case that, to be able to escape today's paralysis, we must include the individual and organisational perspective in our conversation on the transformation of society. These levels are highly interdependent and intricately intertwined. There is no societal transformation without individual transformation. Or, to put it positively, individual transformation has the potential to initiate and catalyse societal dynamics of transformation. The same goes for organisations. Ultimately, they are nothing but platforms for collaboration. As such, they mirror the state of the individuals that 'make' them, just as they have the potential to initiate processes of individual transformation. They serve as laboratories for social innovation that potentially fuels the creation of new patterns at the level of society. At the same time, of course, the transformation of societal structures and dynamics creates ripple effects at both the individual and organisational levels.

Yet when you go to a bookstore and look for books that take an integrated approach to transformation, you will hardly find any. Indeed, the transformation of individuals, organisations, and society usually, is neatly compartmentalised into distinct categories. Individual transformation can be found in the self-help department. The transformation of organisations gets dealt with as a business issue, while the transformation of society is being put onto the bookshelves of the politics and society department.

Over the past years, I have become more and more convinced that this approach is a mistake. We must make an effort to integrate our perspectives and experiences when it comes to individual, organisational and societal transformation. This insight has grown during the past 15 years or so. In that time, I worked in various federal political institutions and joined a political think tank in Berlin, focusing on the transformation of democracy and democratic politics. Ten years ago, I started working as organisational consultant. This role enabled me to facilitate and witness processes of organisational transformation, mostly in the private sector. My most interesting projects focused on increasing the degree of self-organisation in teams and organisations as a whole. These experiments with new models of collaboration and leadership made me understand that, ultimately, organisations are the ideal place to prototype solutions that are needed in society as a whole: models for a different kind of collaboration, deliberation, decision-making. Models that enable human beings to unleash their potential, while increasing their ability to create new solutions with people who think and behave differently than they do – solutions that help us to navigate in an environment that feels less and less stable.

Most importantly, while gathering these experiences in the world of politics and organisational development, I transformed myself. Over the course of the past years, my consciousness changed: the way I look at the world, how I perceive and interpret reality, how I structure my thoughts and actions – and how I ascribe meaning to all this. In this process of unlearning and reconfiguring myself, my perspective on the transformation of social systems changed. I understood that who and how I am has considerable influence on the dynamic in the systems I am part of. My transformation influenced not only those who are dear and close to me. It also enabled me to set more impactful impulses in the organisations I worked with, and gave my political activism a different kind of perspective, stamina and visibility.

During this time, not only did I come to understand that the transformation of individuals and organisations mirrors and influences the transformation of society, but I also realised that there are parallels in how individuals, organisations and society go through processes of transformation. This is especially valid for the early steps of transformation: the steps that precede the letting go of those patterns that hinder us from moving into a more purposeful and meaningful direction, be it individually, as organisations or as society.

These insights alone would not have been enough to write this book. Ultimately, the times we live in made me sit down and write these pages. Mainstream politics may still be obsessed with incremental innovation, while mainstream businesses still talk about change. Yet the climate crisis inevitably drives us towards a fundamental unlearning of some of the patterns that, as of today, constitute who we think we are. We are pushed towards rethinking the frame of the human-made world as we know it: to transform the way we organise the economy, the way politics is being done, and so on. This is why transformation, as a buzzword, is becoming increasingly visible in public discourse. It differs from 'change', in that transformation asks us to go beyond the surface; to reconsider the deeper patterns that make us, to acknowledge and unlearn them, and to replace them with more meaningful ones. While change and incremental politics is about optimising the system within its given boundaries, transformation aims to reconfigure the systemic frame itself.

3x3: the structure of this book

This book's aim is to enable you to take an integrated perspective on transformation. Ideally, it will deepen your understanding of what transformation means at an individual, an organisational and a societal level, and of how these levels are interdependent. You may realise already that this is quite a vast scope. Accordingly, this book chooses a fragmentary approach, with a carefully chosen focus, consciously omitting much that could be discussed as well.

Unlearn is intentionally called a compass, not map, handbook or manual. The following pages are supposed to enable you to take a strategic perspective on transformation, enabling you to find an overall sense of orientation. The hope is that this book's chapters will help you reflect on and expand your perspective while deepening your understanding of transformation on all three levels, thus making it possible for you to deduce insights and approaches that fit your life's situation and environment.

I consciously avoided making this a theoretical book. Transformation is the ultimate human challenge. It deserves an approach that is both emotionally tangible and within the realms of our everyday reality. This is why this book will tell stories, especially in Parts I and II. These stories serve as a fundament for the abstract points the book tries to make, thus making them more accessible. Aspects of these stories are very personal, particularly those in Part I, where I will share some experiences from my journey of transformation. Obviously, such a story is never an end in itself. I chose them simply because I can talk about my own transformation with the greatest authority. They serve to make an overall point which, hopefully, will help you to take a different perspective on your individual journey of unlearning.

By starting with a very personal take on individual transformation, *Part I* invites the reader to develop a personal understanding of *individual transformation* and its challenges. In the first three chapters, you will learn about some basic terms and concepts that will be important for understanding the book's subsequent parts: the idea of unlearning, the learned self, and the core self, especially. *Part II* expands the focus on *organisations*, and how they are important levers for both individual and societal transformation, enabling individuals to create impact that goes beyond what they could achieve on their own. *Part III* discusses the *societal* challenge of unlearning – and what might help us to collectively let go of patterns that, as of today, keep us from moving towards a better future.

All three parts are structured around a set of three perspectives, divided into three chapters. The first perspective looks at *patterns that hold us down*, and thus keep us stuck in the status quo, be it individually, as organisations or as society. Acknowledging and understanding these patterns is the prerequisite for starting a process of unlearning, and thus transforming. The second focuses on how individuals, organisations or society can develop a *sense of the new*, thus cultivating an understanding that a different existence is possible. Lastly, the third perspective dives into exemplary *levers that help us transform*, be it individually, as organisations or society. By levers, I mean interventions that help individuals, organisations or society experience that it is possible to break with learned patterns. They are measures, in other words, that can be cultivated as access points for deeper processes of transformation.

This book is built on the idea that the transformation of individuals and organisations is a means to further the meaningful transformation of society as a whole. Yes, individual or organisational transformation can be self-serving. But all development gains direction, force and impact if it takes the well-being of the greater whole as a focus point. This is what makes sure that we honour our place within the greater systems we are part of, and improve our existence by contributing to something that transcends our individual well-being, or the short-term interests of our organisations.

This also explains why this book focuses on the democratic societies of the global North, even though other parts of the world must change course as well. Firstly, I see the democratic societies of the West as source of the existential trouble the world is in. The cultures of Western democracies have been, since their modern beginning, deeply intertwined with a history of ecological and social exploitation, which makes abandoning this path harder than in other parts of the world. Secondly, the conditions for transformation in, for instance, the democratic societies of Europe are vastly different from those in China or India. Western democracies cultivated a degree of societal self-organisation which, potentially, can be a great asset for the transformation that lies ahead. Thirdly, these are the systems and cultures I know best, and where I feel I can make a difference.

A radical approach: towards Part I

In Latin, roots is *radix*, which is the origin for the word radical. This book aims to take a radical perspective, focusing on the fundament of who we have become, and how we must change this fundament in order to head towards a more meaningful direction. So this is not a book on how we can lead a more sustainable life. This is about how we can start the process of becoming someone else. This is about questioning our roots and transforming the self we cultivated in the past. Obviously, one of the outcomes of this process must be a more sustainable, just society. But this can only be done if we also manage to become a more reflective and empathetic one, one that relates: both to its complexity within, and this beautiful web of complexity we are a product of.

All the qualities mentioned above can only be given life if we realise them on an individual level, through daily practice. This is why this book starts – and ends – with a focus on individual transformation. Individual transformation is, contrary to what most self-help guides tell you, never an end in itself. It is a lever for initiating and catalysing the transformation of the systems we are part of. This is where we both initiate and deepen the transformation of society as a whole. This is where we can achieve the most radical results, creating substance for the transformation of what is around us.

Part I

Individual Transformation

Part I

1 Core Knowledge
The future within us (sensing the new – i)

Scene 1: sensing my otherness

IMAGINE THIS: you are a boy, around eight or nine years old. After school, you play with a good friend at his house. Your friend shows you a box full of costumes, and you decide to dress up with him. A few minutes later, both of you are wearing women's clothes: dresses, headscarves, tights. You look at yourself in the mirror and are amazed by what you see. Both you and your friend have transformed, from boys to something more delicate. You feel that this makes a different way of being possible: kinder, softer, quieter.

You go to your friend's mother for her to take a picture. You take up your position against the hedge, right in front of their house. She looks at you through the lens. Your friend makes faces, opens his mouth wide, goes crazy. You don't. You stand still, because you feel gracious and elegant.

The woman looks up and abruptly tells you: 'You like this too much.'

You instantly know:

She is right

She is dangerous

She knows.

But you don't know what she knows, because you can't. You're just a child.

You don't know why she is dangerous, because you can't. But you do know, and you avoid her from then on.

And you don't know what she is right about, but you know she is.

How could I comprehend transgressing boundaries when no one ever explained to me what they were? How could I smell a predator when I couldn't know that someone might consider me prey? And how could I know I was different before even knowing what sexuality was?

Scene 2: letting go of my life

Around two decades later, I was in my late twenties. Berlin. I was working as a freelance communications consultant. For the first time, I had won a corporate client. Many people told me: this was my moment. To grow my business, to earn, to become more visible with what I did.

It was a summer day in August, an early morning. I went swimming, as I did every morning. The sun was shining; it was one of those Berlin summer days when the city vibrates with heat. But I couldn't so much as feel the warmth of the sunshine on my skin. Worn out. Exhausted. Frustrated. The people in my life lauded my professional achievements, and, for the first time, I earned good money. Yet I felt stressed, overwhelmed, emptied.

I jumped into the clear, cold blue water, crawled length after length when, suddenly, I knew: this is not it. Out of nothing, nothing except my constant movement through the clear water, knowledge emerged. From one moment to the other, my mind shifted, and I understood: I must stop. Quit the clients. Quit this kind of life. There is more to it than all this.

Between one moment and the next, something fundamental had shifted. The veil that had shaded my life for many months lifted, for a precious moment. I felt awake, full of clarity. A crystalline moment. I knew: this inner voice is not a mere idea. This is knowledge.

In a moment, I resolved to let go of the life I had built. I trusted my inner voice, though it ran against all the patterns I had cultivated in my life until that point. Patterns that told me to never subvert external expectations, to never quit commitments, to never exchange safety for insecurity. I knew that I had to let go of all that, though I had no idea what for. I opted for the alternative, although I didn't know what the alternative could possibly be. Because my future had spoken to me with unmistakeable clarity.

Within days, I called most of my clients and told them that I would no longer be working for them. The consequence was losing 80 per cent of my monthly income, without knowing what I would replace it with. At a stroke, I wiped out the professional existence I had built for four years. I was left standing with little savings, little of anything save a feeling of disorientation and utmost loneliness. All this I did without having mapped out viable alternatives, without having a safety net.

From today's perspective, I see that this was the necessary step in making the life I lead today possible. By letting go of the everyday life that was tearing me down, I created space for new ideas, new experiences. Right at that moment, though, I didn't know all this. Indeed, for some months after my decision, I was haunted by a fear that, by letting go of that everyday life, I had given in to the depression and exhaustion that had been there all the time, waiting to take over the steering wheel. For years, I had fought the tendrils of this, by keeping myself frantically busy from dawn to dusk.

Now, with the business gone, the veil that had always been with me expanded, creating a perfect isolation of terrible dullness. I felt caught in cycles of greyness: numb, helpless. An intense fatigue made it impossible for me to imagine finding the energy to create something better than the awfulness of my days back then. Life felt like an intensifying cycle of pointless suffering. Things became so bad that, one day, I realised that, if this is what life is, I don't want it.

Yet despite the terror, I knew that going back to the life I had abandoned in the swimming pool was not an option. I *knew* that turning my back on it had been the right thing to do. Somehow, I trusted the inner voice I had heard in the swimming pool. I had no evidence for it from my former life, but as sure as the inner voice that had conveyed danger to me in my friend's garden, I knew the truth of what it told me in the swimming pool: that there *must* be more to life.

Core knowledge: a model

These two stories of my life might seem very different. Different phases in my life, different causal conditions, and utterly different consequences. Yet, on a deeper level, they both encapsulate the ultimate, miraculous fundament of individual transformation. In both moments, certainty emerged within me. It was knowledge about my future life though, at those points in my biography, it was knowledge that should have been inaccessible to me. Years later, having made the knowledge a reality, I would know it all made sense. But the moment I made a commitment to follow this knowledge, I could not possibly, logically, know what I knew. And still, in both moments, I did. My future had spoken to me, enabling me to know things that, until then, were far from being knowable.

I call this miracle *core knowledge*. It is the fundament and anchor point of every individual transformation: the future that lies within us, calling out to us from deep inside ourselves. When core knowledge speaks to us, it is different from the usual thoughts that occupy our mind all day: deeper, far more intense, fundamental. As if our core self is calling to us from a future place we usually cannot access; a pull towards a more genuine life, even if nothing in our past experience affirms that life can be so.

I understand core knowledge as a powerful gravitational force that, throughout our lives, pulls us in the right direction. A fundamental yet subtle knowledge we all bear inside ourselves, about what is right for us, and which kind of life is true to ourselves. In a way, core knowledge works like an elastic: the further you move away from a life that is in alignment with your core self, the more intensely core knowledge will be sending you signals to change direction. These signals can emerge in different ways: on the one hand, as feelings of physical and mental discomfort, using signals from our entire system to make us understand that we are in the wrong place; and on the other, as the two stories from the beginning of this chapter show, in rare moments core knowledge emerges as a clear message, orientating us at the times we truly need it.

Core knowledge is a spiritual idea. There can be no factual evidence for it. It is individual inner experience on a most existential level. It implies the assertion that certain things in life defy rational explanation and analysis. At the same time, it reminds us that deep human transformation is something that transcends the realms of the logical, and, in its essence, is intricately linked with the deep, mysterious sides of our lives.

As a concept, core knowledge reminds us that certain traits of implicit knowledge are an essential part of the universal human experience. Fundamental traits, accessible and yet autonomous; things which lie within every one of us, and still are beyond the physical world. We all have it, serving as a guide to our own future. What differs is how much we refine our sense of it. It can be a stronger or weaker guidance, depending on how we cultivate the senses that help access it, how much we trust this gravitational force, and how truly we manage to follow it during our life's journey.

The learned self and the core self

What core knowledge pulls us towards is an essence which is unique and timeless. An essence that grounds and defines us, throughout all our life's transformation. It is the source of core knowledge. I will call it *core self* throughout this book. It is something that is *there*, unbound by the environment around us. It precedes and outlasts the creation of our life's transient, changing identity. The core self thus is not something we create; all we can do is refine our sense of it and align with it during our lifetime.

In contrast to the core self, we have our time-bound ego: the entity that we can, and constantly do, adapt and develop. I will call it *learned self*. Understanding the difference between these two selves we carry around is the essential work of self-transformation. While the learned self can potentially be harmful for our well-being, the core self is always in the right place. It is the innermost part of our being. It is unsocial, as it is timeless. It is like a distillate of what we are, which also means that it is unbound by time, culture and convention.

The learned self, on the other hand, is time-bound. It is the self we learn to be – patterns that are not ours, but merely something we integrate as part of our self. As children, adolescents and young adults, over and over again we learn what we are supposed to do and who we are expected to be, be it by our family, peer group or the institutions we are part of. We learn which kinds of behaviour are acceptable in our cultures and social environments, and which are considered inappropriate. This has an important functional aspect to it. The learned self helps us to fit in. However, it also comes with a downside. The patterns we learn to accept as ours are not necessarily aligned with our core. By fulfilling expectations of the world around us, we easily lose touch with it.

Yet as I tried to show with my two stories, there is core knowledge. This inner voice helps us towards closer alignment with our core. As our core self lies at a place we cannot reach, we need core knowledge, and the signals it sends us, to navigate closer to our essence. While it generally pulls us in the right direction, it is by no means an exact force navigating us on a predetermined path towards a goal that is set. What it does is give us a general sense of direction, through messages that can be more or less subtle, more or less painful, more or less specific. It helps us navigate in the vast territories of the unknown we call life.

The voice of core knowledge can emerge in many different ways. Generally, the further our learned self carries us away from our core, the louder core knowledge speaks. To stay with my example, I understand today that core knowledge sent me messages not only through the clear kind of knowing I described in my two stories. On a more uncomfortable level, the depressions and physical pains I carried with me for years were also early and permanent signals to change direction. All these signals ran against what my learned self told me to do: keep going, carry on. They told me to exchange the discomfort of the known for the uncertainties of the unknown. To start exploring a life that, while completely alien to me, would lead me closer towards my core.

I visualise this dynamic using the model in Figure 1. The *learned self*, in the middle, is the time-bound result of *the known*, or the past. It is the self we learned to be as a result of our past experiences. Ahead of the learned self lies *the unknown*. This, basically, is our future, with its limitless options. From deep within our unknown future, on the right side of this visualisation, the core self pulls us towards the unknown via messages of various kinds, which we can choose to listen to, or not. This core is our real essence, stripped naked of convention, compliance and the need to please.

The learned self is constantly drawn in different directions, attracted both by core knowledge and the external influences of the known. Just as our core is sending us signals that lead us towards it, our past and the patterns we have learned have a powerful impact on our learned self and its decision-making. They anchor us in the learned self, with all its patterns, be they productive or destructive for us.

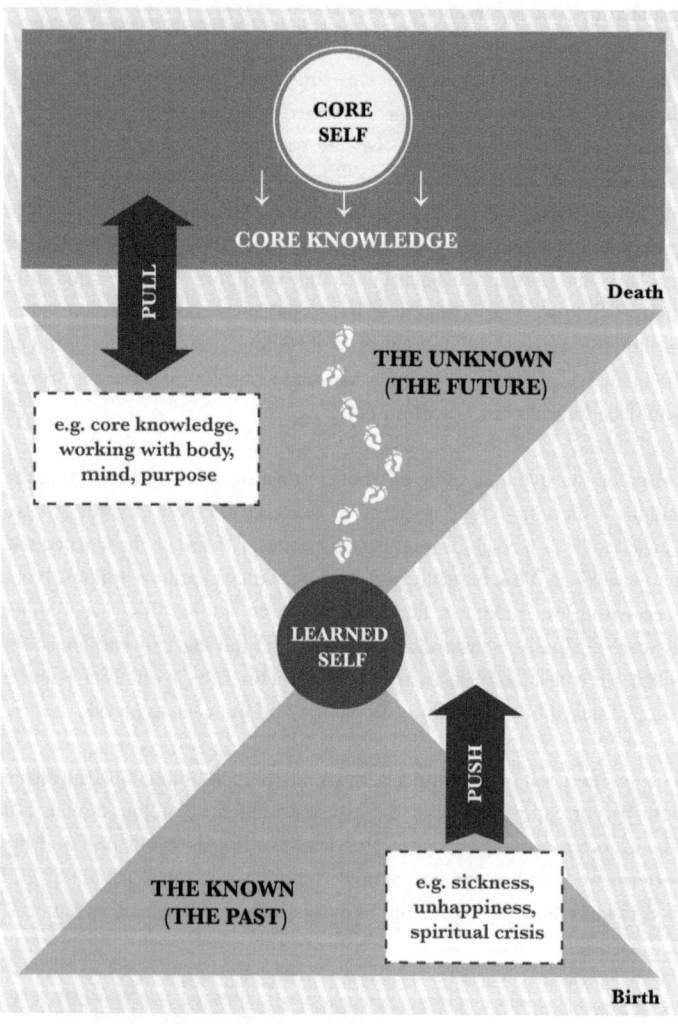

Figure 1 Individual Transformation

The discomfort of entering the unknown

Heeding the call of the core self is rarely easy or simple. To go back to my story, even after my revelation in the swimming pool, I didn't know what to do; I had no conception that I could unlearn so many of the learned patterns that were making me sad, lonely and tired. Yet I did have the core knowledge in me that a different life was possible. What I did not know was what that meant, and how I would get there.

Indeed, taking a leap into the unknown, and in so doing, choosing not to fulfil my external commitments and expectations, came with a huge amount of psychological resistance. My learned self warned me against doing what I did. I was afraid, doubtful and often angry. While I knew that I had to change, everything I had learned so far told me not to; to stay in the known instead of exploring the unknown.

I believe this encapsulates an attitude we all learn as a default. To continue living the life we learned to live, even when it clearly makes us feel unwell. To endure suffering, on whatever level it may be, and to spend tremendous amounts of energy on fighting the symptoms our core self sends us, as a signal and an invitation to transform. We prefer sticking to what is predictable, even a state of perpetual unease, rather than entering the uncertainty of the unknown. We are far more willing to be hurt by what we know, than to face the fear of what we may suffer while exploring unknown territories. Paradoxically, fear of something that has not happened yet seems far more powerful than real pain in the here and now.

It is remarkable how well humans perform when it comes to ignoring their pain, and the message contained within it, and so hold on to self-destructive patterns affecting their everyday lives. Ultimately, though, pain and suffering can have a highly productive function: to push us out of the discomfort of the status quo, be it towards a different perspective on life, or a different life altogether. I think of my own example. It took me almost 30 years until, following my episode in the swimming pool, I seriously started to tackle the deeper roots of my suffering. For my whole life up until that point, I harboured the strong sense that unhappiness and suffering were simply a given. This perception in turn caused me to cultivate a mindset of negativity and fatalism. In a way, I became a victim of myself. Not because I had bad intentions, but because I did not know better.

The individual experience of transformation

Once I did start to move towards a new place, it felt as if things got worse, not better. Prior to that point, I may have been unwell. But in my unhappiness, at least I knew what to expect. Now, sitting alone in my apartment, I did not know anything any more. I was in the deep unknown, completely lost and very afraid. Only later did I fully understand that this moment of disorientation was unavoidable. Indeed, disorientation and the discomfort it causes are something we can count on in phases of transformation. It is a consequence of the reconfiguration of our lives, and thus our learned selves. As part of this, we experience insecurity and fear; we have the impression of chaos. We are torn between the ambivalence of the old, which promises both pain and a sense of security, and the new, which, though holding the potential for something better, feels threatening.

This negative double-bind is what makes the individual experience of transformation so hard. The known is sticky. You never know when the shift from the status quo to something new will happen. This can be deeply uncomfortable; the insecurity of the unknown feels a lot scarier than the known pains we have grown used to. In fact, the discomfort of unlearning old patterns can be so hard that you will wonder: why am I doing this? Are all these efforts worth it? In these moments, it may well be far from obvious that you are making any progress whatsoever. This easily results in a reflex to favour the status quo ante, and thus to abort steps of transformation even after we have begun them.

The disorientation and discomfort we feel are a constitutive part of our journey. We are afraid, insecure, sometimes hopeless. In my experience, this moment feels like staggering into an endless field of thick, grey fog. While we may sense that the general direction is right, we do not know where exactly we need to go, and what we will encounter along the way. We cannot run, we risk falling in the sightless terrain. Not wanting to turn back, we must take it bit by bit, slowly shuffling forward into the new, exploring its vastness cautiously, adapting our course on the way.

This step-by-step approach makes it possible for us to adjust, even to go one step back at times. Indeed, I experienced my own transformation as a sequence of small decisions: I walked, assessed, adjusted. Until one day, to my great surprise, I realised that things had substantially changed. By reconfiguring my life little by little, day by day, I transformed. I moved towards a new inner place until I noticed: this is different from how it used to be. The fog of the unknown had lifted, unveiling the new terrains of a different life.

Individual transformation is characterised by this asynchronicity. On the one hand, it takes time. Constant effort and small steps are what builds its fundament. This pace may look hesitant in retrospect. Yet as we walk it, it feels demanding, pushing our limits. At the same time – and this is what makes it asynchronous – transformation is deeply non-linear. The shift towards the new happens when it happens. And when it does, it takes you to a different stage in your life that brings with it a shift of consciousness: the way we perceive and interpret reality, how we structure our thoughts and actions, and how we ascribe meaning to all this. This shift cannot be undone – which makes transformation a radical way to permanently change our world.

Transformation and stages of consciousness development

Transformation is the essence of life, a continuous process both within and around us. Our bodies are fluid structures, in cycles of complete renewal and permanent reconfiguration of wonderful complexity. We are embedded in the gigantic life web of the ecosystem, a web that constantly transforms and, in that process, re-structures itself. And we are part of human society, which has rapidly and radically transformed its size, way of life and governance within our recent memory, and continues to do so. Individually, we live lives that are marked by transformative events: birth, the 24/7 crisis of puberty, the rebuilding of our lives as adults, birth of children, the physical experience of ageing and, ultimately, dying.

Yet while life's transformation is constant, the transformation of our consciousness knows a different rhythm; it happens in shifts. One helpful model to understand this can be found in the work of Robert Kegan, a developmental psychologist. In his research, he describes stages of individual consciousness development. A person's developmental stage determines how they structure the reality they perceive, how they react to it and the kind of identity they construct around it. Kegan sees five stages of human consciousness:

> **Impulsive (I)**: We all pass through this stage as small children. Individuals who act from an impulsive level of consciousness are what they perceive. They build their lives around the impulses they feel. They do what they feel like – full stop.
>
> **Imperial (II)**: At this stage, we are motivated by our needs and desires. Our major aim is to make the world do what we want. People are mostly means to ends as defined by our self-interest. When we operate from this consciousness level, we are motivated by external rewards – and punishment. Even though most people transcend this stage during early adolescence, around 6 per cent of the adult population function according to this stage.
>
> **Socialised (III)**: The socialised stage of consciousness is interpersonal and oriented towards higher authority. Our behaviour is oriented towards satisfying the norms and expectations of the group we are part of, be it family, our employer or a group of friends. Accordingly, we think a lot about what others want and expect, instead of asking ourselves what is right and good for ourselves. On this level, we learn to discipline the interests, desires and needs that governed us in the imperial stage. This enables us to comply with outside norms and fulfil external expectations. It makes it possible to fit in, to feel part of a family, a group of friends or colleagues. According to Kegan's research, around 60 per cent of adults operate from this consciousness level.
>
> **Self-authoring (IV)**: Only around a third of the adult population acts from a self-authoring consciousness. These people

are not, as in the socialised stage, oriented towards external authorities, expectations and norms. Self-authoring individuals have the capability to align their behaviour with their inner compass, instead of being fixated on one that is externally defined (by their parents, boss, friends…). While they know how to move successfully in social systems – which they learned during the socialised stage – their higher purpose and values, when in doubt, trump the needs and wants of their peer group. Accordingly, self-authoring individuals have a developed sense of inner guidance. Being liked becomes secondary to doing the right thing. When in doubt, they have firm values and a general sense of orientation, through the higher purpose they defined for themselves. This enables them to design their own, potentially unconventional way of living their life.

Self-transcending (V): People who operate from a self-transcending consciousness understand that their very self is something fluid. Therefore, they adapt their identity to serving the higher needs they see in the world around them. These individuals – only 1 per cent of the population – are capable of dynamic and frequent perspective taking while still having a firm personal sense of direction and rootedness. They are at peace with who they are and understand that they are an instrument for achieving something which transcends them. While they know about outside norms and inside patterns, they cultivate a playful relationship with these potential limitations.

While all five consciousness levels are potentially available to us, in reality we know that the higher the level, the fewer the individuals acting from it. Every one of us experiences the impulsive stage as an infant. As children, we all operate from an imperial stage, heavily focused on satisfying our immediate needs and making our environment do what we want. During early adolescence, most people – more than 90 per cent – transition to a socialised mindset, and the majority operate from this level for the rest of their lifetime. Those who master the transformation towards a self-authoring consciousness usually do so during the so-called mid-life crisis, (i.e. in the late thirties to early forties).

When we transition into a higher stage of consciousness, we still embody the earlier stages. We may operate stably from, let us say, a socialised mindset. Yet when under intense negative stress, we can make use of the abilities we developed when mainly operating from an imperial level of consciousness. The stages Kegan describes thus have nothing to do with the kind of intelligence that is measured via an IQ test. Many people who, from the IQ perspective, are very intelligent, operate from an imperial or socialised mindset until they die.

The transition from one consciousness level to the next is of an evolutionary nature. People must necessarily go through the first three stages before being able to operate from the self-authoring stage. The pace of this development depends on the environment we live in. Most people, whether 30, 50 or 70 years old, will never act from a self-authoring or self-transcending level of consciousness. By contrast, some people – in particular those lucky enough to grow up in a safe, caring and nurturing environment supportive of their development – can achieve a stable self-authoring mindset in their twenties. Unfortunately, the institutional worlds most of us live in (kindergartens, schools, universities, the workplace) reinforce an imperial and socialised mindset, and tend to give individuals with a self-authoring mindset a hard time.

We will go back to Kegan's model in Chapters 5 and 6. What we should note here is that the hardships of transformation I wrote about above are the necessary by-product of evolving from one stage of consciousness to the next. Thinking of my own transformative crisis, it seems plausible that I transitioned from a socialised to a self-authoring mindset. Stated in this way, this transition sounds very structured and orderly. But this wasn't the case at all. I vividly remember how messy, disorientating and existentially demanding this phase of my life was. After all, switching from one consciousness level to the next entails paradigmatic transformation in almost all dimensions of life. We alter how we perceive the world around us, and our place in it, and thus destabilise what used to be stable previously. This is crucial to keep in mind. We can structure the transformation of humans and human systems in orderly models, which can be very helpful. But what these models should never disguise or distract us from is that the hardship transformation brings is an integral part of developing towards a better place in our lives.

Unlearning who we are

If our aim is to grow and develop, gaining a clear understanding of the patterns that guide our learned self – our pull backwards, to recall the earlier model – is crucial. These are the patterns we learned to accept as ours in our earlier lives, but which keep us from aligning more closely with our core. Only by fully seeing and understanding them can we take a conscious step back, reflecting on which ones to keep and which ones to unlearn. This kind of unlearning requires insight not just into our individual past but into our collective one: the intricate ways each of us are interwoven with our family's and society's history – how the past continues to make our present, so to speak, if we let it.

2 Unlearning
Letting go of who we learned to be
(the patterns that hold us down – i)

THROUGHOUT OUR lives, we develop mechanisms for coping with the environment we live in. As children and teenagers, we do so in a world that is hegemonic. For most of us, there is no alternative to the reality we grow up in. Both its blessings and its terrors we learn to think of as normal. As children, we adapt to what we believe the world to be, necessarily ignorant of the fact that the creation of a different reality, a different life, is a genuine option. Only later, as adults, can we learn to consciously see who we have become, and unlearn the parts of our selves we decide not to carry into the future.

In the last chapter I shared a point of crisis that propelled me towards transforming myself, and thus my life. As I realised during that transformation, becoming someone else – entering the unknown and exploring new territories – required the conscious letting go of patterns that I had learned to think of as 'me' during my childhood and youth. Patterns which, as we will see in this chapter, are rooted in the heritage that society and my family provided me with, defining my mental and physical learned self for many years.

In this chapter, I will focus on how Germany's totalitarian past shaped my family's patterns, and thus my learned self. The worldviews, beliefs and behaviours they came with were developed in the past, in lives that were not mine. Yet these branches of history ran through me and defined me. Letting them go was a prerequisite for defining a life that is in closer alignment with my core self.

Despite the Germanness of my story, it is important to emphasise that the dynamic it describes is not bound to specific social systems. The story I tell could be told by any citizen of any nation, knowing that, while the narrative may sound different, its core stays the same.

Individuals as fractals

Our learned self is 'made' by patterns we adopt and perpetuate, in most cases unconsciously. In one way or another, every human and every social system is both blessed and cursed with patterns we inherited from the past. Whatever the specifics of our ancestral and cultural heritage, it is clear that every one of us – wherever we are from – is deeply influenced by the family and the society we were brought up within. These shape us. That person we have learned to become thus reflects the larger systems we are part of; we are a *fractal* of something that is bigger than us. We mirror what we are part of. And what we are part of mirrors what we are. It is an intricate dynamic we will repeatedly go back to during the course of this book. While we cannot avoid being shaped, we have the opportunity to actively reshape parts of our learned self in our adult lives. We can consciously choose which patterns we aim to strengthen through our existence.

By being who we are, we catalyse and reinforce mindsets, norms and behaviours. This is what makes the conscious reflection of who we have learned to be so important. If we fail to stop, reflect and unlearn, we are very likely to perpetuate learned patterns that are harmful: to us, to our family and friends, and to society. Patterns that may run against our core, and thus what we truly aim to strengthen in this world. I call this conscious reconfiguration of who we are *unlearning*; the process of detecting and acknowledging the learned patterns that negatively shape us and our actions, and the conscious act of letting them go. This is the work that core knowledge nudges us towards: sorting through who we have learned to be, and letting go of who we decide to not be any more. In doing so, we actively choose who we want to be in this world, and thus which kind of world we aim to further.

The roots: a story from a past not mine

Let us dive deeper into this by exploring a story that made me, well into my adult life, identify and acknowledge patterns that are not mine, and unlearn them. This story begins with my grandmother.

During one of my visits – I was around 20 years old – we went for a drive up the Swabian Alps. Navigating through curvy serpentines, my grandma, who was born in 1922, suddenly started talking about a cousin of hers. As she told me while driving through the autumn landscape, her cousin – born 1916, six years older than my grandmother – was 'mentally disturbed'. The girl had fits, and, in my grandma's words, 'sexually attacked' men of all ages, hugging them and grabbing their genitals, 'embarrassing everyone around her'. In the early 1930s, my grandmother's uncle sent his teenage daughter to a psychiatric clinic. There, my grandmother told me, her cousin died in 1940. 'My uncle was devastated,' she said, eyes straight ahead on the road. 'But maybe it was better this way.' After a short, excruciating pause, she continued talking about her uncle, and said no more about her cousin.

I remember sitting in the car, filled with both a sense of shock and subsequent fear. I was horrified by how my grandmother talked about her cousin's death, but automatically caught myself with a reflex I had known since my early childhood: to refrain from inquiring, to suppress my emotions and to silently endure my intense discomfort with what she had told me. I sat still, hoping the unease would pass, and with it the dissonance between the said and unsaid.

Years later, my father shed new light on this story. Like me, he had only heard my grandmother's version of it. Moved to finally find out about our late relative's fate, he drove to Bethel, the church-owned psychiatric clinic where my grandma's cousin had been institutionalised. It's still active today, with all their historical records available. My father discovered a neat stack of documents on my grandmother's cousin. They had sat there for decades, waiting for someone to enquire what had happened to her. In 76 years since her death, nobody had come.

As my dad found out during his research, my grandma's cousin Ursula first came to Bethel when she was 16 years old. Her father reported fits and seizures Ursula had had since she was eight. Overall, though, Bethel's first report on Ursula states that 'the sickness can be cured, as the seizures seem to be caused by the patient's psychopathic inclinations. The educational moment will foreseeably play the biggest role [in curing her] ... On first sight, patient gives impression of a healthy person. Is well-oriented.'

As the months passed, however, the notes show the psychiatric institution's focus quickly shifted, from the aim of helping Ursula towards an increasingly harsh pathologisation of her character. Ursula's fits – the reason why she was institutionalised in the first place – are mentioned very rarely in her doctors' reports. Rather, the written remarks talk about Ursula's behaviour. She secretly read books at night, slept longer than allowed and got into quarrels with patients and the staff. Reading the doctors' notes from today's perspective, Ursula, refusing to accommodate herself in the forced isolation of psychiatry, showed what anyone would think of as normal teenager behaviour.

Not in the Nazi world, though. The doctors' files show open hostility towards the patient, reflecting the norms of German society, which were increasingly unforgiving when it came to non-conformism. Both state and staff took ever more severe measures against the teenager. In 1936, the reports note the decision of the Hereditary Health Court to enforce

Ursula's sterilisation, which happened shortly later, followed by severe complications over more than two months. In 1938, Ursula was ordered to be moved to Merxhausen, a provincial state psychiatric unit in southern Germany. The files become yet more sparse. In early 1940, just months after her forced sterilisation, they note 'an enormous loss of weight'. In March, fever and diarrhoea. One week later, a letter informs Ursula's father of his daughter's death. She was buried without any relatives present.

As my father's research shows, Ursula, like many others, had been starved to death, her reported sickness being physical symptoms of months-long undernourishment. The Nazi administration had constantly reduced the spending on mental institutions, especially for inmates, like Ursula, who were considered unfit for labour. At the same time, the number of patients per institution massively increased while the number of staff did not, which led to systemic neglect. When Ursula died, four doctors were responsible for 1,300 inmates in the Merxhausen institution.

It is a horrendous synchronicity of things. While my grandmother climbed the ranks in the Hitler Youth and, with thousands of other young Nazis, enthusiastically greeted Joseph Goebbels in Nuremberg, her cousin was being incarcerated, sterilised and killed in a psychiatric institution.

What made my grandmother, decades after the official end of the Nazi regime in Germany, continue to repeat the Nazi verdict that Ursula's death 'was better that way'? From the viewpoint of totalitarianism, her perspective made sense. In terms of National Socialist logic, Ursula was a negative deviant, unable to adapt to societal norms and expectations. First her character in life, then the circumstances of her death, had the potential to bring unwanted attention to a family that, like millions of other Germans, excelled at blending into the Nazi system. Ursula's death did not warrant protest, inquiry, discussion – just like the disappearance of my grandmother's Jewish schoolmates, or the incarceration of Communists, Social Democrats, gays and so many others did not. In Nazi Germany, asking the wrong questions was potentially dangerous, both with regards to potential persecution by state authorities and the inner ideological conflicts such questions would have laid bare.

Third-generation collaborator

The death of my grandmother's cousin was not followed by mourning, questions, conflict. An emotional void, even long after the war. For more than 70 years, my family decided to not find out why a family member died in a Nazi institution. For decades, like me sitting silently in my grandmother's car, they listened to fragmented, intuitively violent stories: not inquiring, not voicing doubt. For some reason, three generations decided to accept discomfort and dissonance instead of seeking conflict and clarity.

When, after his trip to Bethel, my father told me about what he had found, I felt guilt and sadness. Why had *I* been silent when my grandmother told me her version of the story? Why hadn't *I* inquired? What had made *me* continue with this familiar pattern of silence – a pattern that enabled my grandmother to maintain her Nazi perspective on what had happened, without any resistance and conflict to speak of? And, most importantly, what part do *I* play in perpetuating exactly those patterns which ran through and animated those horrors?

The longer I reflected on these questions, the more I realised that since early childhood I had learned to evade conflict, to not speak up, to silently blend in. To not acknowledge dissonance, to silence my emotions, to override my intuition. I had learned to dissociate myself from thoughts, emotions and reactions that had the potential to disturb the peace in my family. A peace so fragile and silently violent that I intuitively knew how little it would take to break it.

The more I thought about it, the more I understood how deeply influenced I had been by my family's totalitarian heritage; how, through the first three decades of my life, I had replicated a totalitarian identity my family had cultivated decades before my birth. I came to realise that most of the patterns I had learned at home are perfectly suited for living in a dictatorship without ever being bothered:

- please others – fulfil other people's expectations

- accept authority and external norms – no deviance

- get a sense of what the other person wants before you speak out or act

- do not warrant attention when in public – avoid risks

- blend into the majority – deviate only when you can be better than them

- distrust – expect people to be willing to hurt you.

Born almost four decades after the fall of Nazi Germany, I had been equipped, by my family, with patterns that were tailored towards making yourself fit in to a totalitarian system. As my family's history shows, by blending in – and, in parts, by actively supporting – they lived unharmed. The person who deviated from this pattern – Ursula – died.

As I confronted these principles ingrained in me, I saw how the behavioural defaults I learned as a child are also the traits of the perfect 'Mitläufer', or collaborator. At first, I was tempted to blame my parents for raising me the way they did. Yet I understood that, just like me, they were subjected to patterns that reach back beyond their conscious life choices. The way they brought me up mirrors the overall patterns they learned to see as normal in their own childhoods. Like mine, their learned selves mirrored patterns their parents and grandparents developed: coping mechanisms for living in Nazi Germany.

Beginning to unlearn

Gaining these insights enabled me to develop a new perspective on the life I had lived as a child, teenager and young man, and the hardships that came with it. I more clearly understood why it had taken me so long to openly live as a gay man. Everything I had learned to be in my young life was directed against expressing this part of me: a part I had clearly felt since a very early age. I now saw why, to go back to the story at the very beginning of Chapter 1, I had had a strong sense since my early childhood that showing myself fully would existentially endanger me. I understood why I had felt so threatened when my childhood friend's mother said what she said. Being seen as different, being singled out as deviant: in the totalitarian logic I had grown up with, this spelled severe danger.

Though core knowledge told me that I was different from the people around me, my learned self dictated how it was imperative to hide this part of my identity, to blend in with what the norm was around me. In this mindset, to ensure an unharmed life, to maintain my family's reputation, I had to make sure I was not truly seen. As a consequence, for many years, I lived a veiled life. I cultivated a self that stayed within the bounds of the unremarkable. Instead of exploring and cultivating what I knew was part of myself, I suppressed and silenced it. Repeating the patterns I had learned at home, passed down through the years and the generations, I unconsciously embraced the idea that showing my true self would have negative consequences. That I would not be loved, protected and nurtured by those around me, but judged and corrected.

As a consequence, I lived a functional life for almost 30 years, dissociated from my core. It was a veiled, silenced kind of a life. Ultimately, it took several crises to make me begin to unlearn the totalitarian patterns that defined my learned self since I was a little child. These crises made me stop and take stock. I acknowledged who I had become, and realised I had a choice. I could continue with what I had learned, prolong my suffering and perpetuate my family's totalitarian patterns. Or alternatively, I could decide these were patterns I wanted to let go, and replace them with ones in closer alignment with my core self.

Breaking with the long lines of history

'So why does this all matter?', you may ask. In my eyes, the answer is simple yet profound: by transforming as individuals, we lay the fundament for transforming the greater systems we are part of.

As we discussed above, my young learned self was a fractal, mirroring the patterns present in my family. At the same time, my family's patterns are a fractal for the patterns of German society as a whole. As we will see again and again in this book, individuals, social systems and societies are deeply interdependent. They mirror, make and unmake each other. Our individual decision whether we perpetuate the patterns of our learned self or not thus reaches far beyond our individual lives. It causes ripple effects for our social environment, and for society as a whole. Just like the transformation of society or organisations causes us to develop individually.

This is why individual unlearning matters, not only for the individual themselves, but also for our collective future. By looking at who we have learned to become, and by acknowledging the factors that made us so, not only do we carry out the groundwork for developing closer towards our core; we also contribute to the breaking down of patterns that are much bigger than ourselves and can, potentially, hold us down collectively. Thus, by transforming on an individual level, we also intervene in the interdependent dynamics with the social systems we are part of.

My story stands as an example for millions of lives. It reminds us that history is something we embody, its long, subtle roots running and living through us every day. Germany, with its despicable past, may be a particularly stark example. Yet at the same time, most countries bear historic burdens that reach into the present in various dimensions. Think of the deep roots of colonialism in countries like Great Britain, the Netherlands and France, or the mass involvement in genocide, slavery and racial segregation in the United States. Wherever you look, you will find traumatising moments in collective history, with grave consequences for how we live as societies – and thus individually – today.

Acknowledging history's footprints on our souls, minds and bodies is crucial for understanding and decoding the patterns that guide us today, and which our ancestors cultivated, in response to environments that were different from ours today. We inherit them, without anyone actively pursuing this, even though the purpose they once served is gone. Over the last years, important research has been put forward on intergenerational trauma and behavioural patterns that cross generational boundaries. The findings of these works are essentially that many of the ills we fight with in our individual lives – mental illness, substance abuse, physical problems – were in our family long before we were born. Whether we perceive it or not, we incorporate and mirror those patterns; even if we, on a cognitive level, do not know about them. This also counts for the way we think, feel and behave.

I believe we need to be aware of these long lines to be able to free ourselves from them. Seeing and acknowledging their presence is the first step towards separating what is truly ours from the burdens others put on our shoulders. It takes time and intense inner work to uncover and unlearn the patterns that result from this long tail of past worlds. But I do believe that we, essentially, have a moral obligation to accept this task of claiming authorship over our own lives, by acknowledging and cutting roots that hold us down, and by replacing them with patterns that are more in line with our core self.

Ultimately, this is the responsibility we all carry, both for the sake of our own lives, and those of the next generations. Our ancestors' negative patterns are not ours to carry, not ours to cultivate, not ours to bequeath to those who follow after us. Facing our family's and our own past, in other words, is not an end in itself. It is the precondition for us to understand which patterns of our learned self we truly want to accept as ours.

The bittersweetness of unlearning

Looking back on recent years, I see a story of unbecoming. A process of unlearning that is by no means a linear one. Often, I was (and am) frustrated by the seeming fruitlessness of my attempts to unlearn negative patterns that are not mine, with a strong sense of being caught in endless cycles of repeatedly stepping into the mental and physical traps I lived in during my younger years. And then, there are these few moments when, suddenly, I realise that something is shifting, that all the loops of frustration are nothing but the fundament for the transformations I experience, and with them the breaking of the totalitarian patterns passed on through generations. This inner work feels like peeling an onion. I advance layer by layer – and yet, whenever I feel I am close to the core, I am confronted with new layers of my learned self I want gone. It is a process of permanent realisation that I will never, no matter the work I have done, be free from negative patterns that I reject as constituting 'me'. The only thing I can do is continue peeling.

I came to appreciate the bittersweet, never-ending nature of this work. I marvel at how many parts of what I considered 'myself' are actually the reflection of earlier generations' experiences, traumas and life choices. Indeed, I realised that there may not be as much 'myself' as I had learned to believe there is. Most parts of my learned self are negotiable, exchangeable – outside layers which, very easily, distract from the core self that truly deserves care, attention and cultivation.

What unlearning requires the most, I believe, is this insight: that most of what we believe we are is actually part of an adaptable vessel, waiting to be transformed. The essence that truly defines us as unique beings is the small, essential core self that, if we take care to listen to it, will always keep us from the nothingness we dread as we let go of parts of the learned self. We are, like everything around us, permanent movement; as humans, we *are* transformation incarnate, and will never be past it.

3 Breaking Barriers
Levers towards the core self
(levers towards the new – i)

IN THE first two chapters, we discussed how crucial unlearning is for meaningful individual transformation. We explored how, to start unlearning, we need some form of core knowledge that pulls us towards our core, and thus the unknown. We learned that, as individuals, we are fractals of the social systems we are part of, be they our family or society. Our individual journey of transformation has repercussions beyond our individual lives; when we unlearn patterns of our learned self, we create ripple effects that have consequences for the world around us.

As we will discuss in this chapter, there are various access points – levers, as I will call them – that help us develop and deepen our understanding of what our core is. These levers enable us to explore the unknown, and catalyse the unlearning of old patterns. They create access points for transformation, by peeling away the skins of the learned self, and thus helping us to get closer to the self we are meant – and want – to be. This chapter introduces three central levers for accessing and refining our sense of our core self:

- firstly, working with the *body*, by identifying and changing physical patterns we carry with us from our earlier life;

- secondly, working with our *mind*, and, through that, beginning to grasp that we are part of a greater whole; and

- the third lever is cultivating our sense of our life's *values and purpose*. This gives meaning and direction to our transformational journey, reminding us that this journey is itself a means to a higher end.

All of these levers are concrete practices, things we can actively do as part of our everyday lives to broaden and catalyse the access to our core. These practices can be found, in various forms and expressions, at the centre of any number of practices, traditions and shared knowledge spanning civilisations and the course of human history. They enable us to initiate and deepen individual transformation. They are not the solution in themselves, but part of the wonderful process of transforming our lives.

Lever 1: unlearning the body

In the Western world, we have inherited an intellectual tradition of the last few centuries which, unfortunately, encourages us to understand the body as something which is separate from both the mind and the world around us, and which is itself separable into its distinct parts. This mechanistic perspective on our physical self severely limits our access to our core self. Once we refine our sense of our body, we realise that it is not only a product of how we move, eat, drink – but that it also holds our past and enables us to access our future. On my own transformative journey, I learned to see my body as intertwined and in constant interconnection with all aspects of myself: my mind, my emotions, my intuition.

The body is inseparable from consciousness, mind and emotions. There is no boundary between them. It is simultaneously an anchor from the present to the past, and a channel to what lies ahead of us. What is important is not so much the body's physical matter, but the reciprocity between our physical self and other aspects of it. Unlearning and transforming how we use our body thus is a highly effective intervention in our entire system, with repercussions that go far beyond the physical.

Throughout our lives, starting at a very early age, we develop physical patterns in reaction to the world we perceive. We learn to take up either a lot or very little space; to be upright or hunched; to open up or close down; to be active or passive; quick or slow. We develop such patterns to cope with the world we encounter. They both express and create our state of mind.

The tricky thing about our physical patterns is that they have a sense of permanence and necessity, often to the point where we cannot imagine anything different and as such cease to really notice them at all. We perceive them as being an integral part of who we are, especially those we developed when we were very young. We hold on to them, even when the environment we developed these patterns for is gone. As a consequence, our enduring physical response, to a world that has itself ceased to be, keeps us locked in the past. When this is the case, our physical patterns, once useful, lower our ability to deal with the contexts we live in *right now*.

To take one example, at a very early point in my life I developed a physical pattern of always being on guard. I never fully relaxed – an expression of an underlying comprehension that something could easily hurt me if I lowered my attention and displayed how I really wanted to be. It was a reaction that was caused by my family's patterns I wrote about in the last chapter. Always being on guard manifested itself physically. My constant degree of alertness expressed itself in permanent muscle tension, shallow breathing and a shutting away of my body. My eyes, my heart, my guts were always shielded, hardened and thus untouchable.

For many years, this physical pattern fulfilled its function. It enabled me both to navigate social environments that felt like a threat to my integrity, and to fulfil social requirements. When I started my adult life, I unintentionally and unconsciously held on to it. I associated my learned physical patterns with myself – and thus carried this physical relic of my younger years with me into my adult life. The lack of inner space. The stiffness in my muscles. My hardened eyes, heart and guts. I had learned to live that way, never realising that the whole way I carried my body could be different. This dawned on me only years later.

At a certain point in my adulthood, I started feeling a permanent, silent and stabbing pain in my back. This was part of a long list of physical dissonances I had come to accept as normal: a colon that seemed to be constantly stiffened and blocked. Neck pains. Migraines. I had the impression that my body was sending me more and more urgent signals: 'Not like this.' I was lucky to find practitioners skilled in identifying and working on the intersection of body and mind. Through working with them I came to realise that I could actively put a stop to the patterns from my earlier life. How eating differently changes my entire state of being. How I can, when I relax my muscles, understand that I am not threatened but positively energised. How, by accepting the presence of the frightened, agonised child in me, I can take care of its desire to be protected without shutting myself down, physically or socially.

These practitioner-supported interventions in my physical patterns showed me it is possible to shift how I feel, even within a couple of minutes. Working on my physical automatisms created cracks of light inside me. I saw and felt how a different state of being is within my reach when I can break through the existing patterns I created in the past. At the same time, I realised how changing my physical state altered the state of my mind – how I could touch deeper parts of myself by concentrating on the physical surface. Working with my body enables me to quickly tune in to core knowledge. In good moments, I receive instant, positive feedback from within when new patterns I experiment with are in closer alignment with my core. Just as the core sends me painful signals when I regress towards a negative place or remain stuck in the status quo.

Just like the development of our consciousness that we discussed in Chapter 1, adopting new physical patterns is a non-linear process. Often, this makes the physical practice of unlearning incredibly frustrating. After all, it is not a simple task to change physical automatisms that we have cultivated for many years, often decades. Letting go of them does not happen overnight. Regression into the old is thus part of the process. These steps backwards are our learned self's response to moving our body into the unknown, and the uncertainty and cluelessness that comes with it. Until, suddenly, we realise that we have shifted into a different place.

Lever 2: unlearning the mind

Just as we have physical patterns that can limit or catalyse us, our learned mental patterns have the potential to either hold us down or productively support us. Accordingly, intervening in how we perceive and think is a powerful lever for accelerating our transformation towards a closer alignment with our core.

As we discussed above, we easily mistake learned physical patterns for something that is essentially 'us', overlooking our capability to actively change them. We treat the mind in similar ways. We learn to understand our mind's voice as essentially 'us'; we imagine it is the voice of 'us' speaking to ourselves. Yet, just like our physical patterns, the patterns of our mind are a result of what we learned in the past. They are a mirror of earlier experience, which, in many cases, makes them a source of suffering, keeping us stuck in a place that serves what has been, instead of what could be.

In my younger life, it never occurred to me that my mind could be anything but positive. Highly rewarded both in my family life and in my school education, my very active mind was my guarantee for a certain degree of autonomy. As long as I managed to excel, I kept unwanted attention away from me. Keeping my head in overdrive kept me safe. As with the physical defences I describe above, this pattern was initially a helpful one.

However, the permanent auto-activity of my mind increasingly haunted me as I grew older. As I understand today, while it was easy for me to rest my body, I grew increasingly unable to rest my mind. I had no sense at all that there was any other way of being than having a mind that was busy all the time. At some point, this inability to truly rest produced a constant sense of feeling drained. My response was to again rest my body, which had no positive effect at all. I was absolutely untouched by the idea that my mind could be the source of my exhaustion.

It took the crisis I wrote about in Chapter 1 to confront this assumption. As one of many experiments I undertook to get better, I started to meditate. To my surprise, I immediately felt the potential relief this practice offered. Though, when I sat and observed what was going on in my mind for the first time, I was shocked by what I found. Informed by the cliché of perfectly peaceful meditation, what I expected to find was calm and stillness. Instead, I was confronted with whirling, relentless, hyperactive thinking. Quickly, I realised that for the most part, these thoughts of mine were not only mostly negative, but also quite superfluous.

Meditation enabled me to acknowledge this pattern of mental negativity in permanent overdrive – the first and most crucial step towards unlearning it. Realising how much my mind's learned patterns actually tormented me was painfully absurd at times. I remember my first week-long silent retreat. When I arrived at the retreat centre, I was curious to see how such an experience would deepen my practice, how I would find some peace. And indeed, physically I found myself in a breathtakingly beautiful landscape. The sound of birdsongs, frogs, crickets and chipmunks, the wind moving the leaves. But my mind did everything it could to escape this beauty. It meticulously planned days that lay in the future, fussed about things from the past, and spent great amounts of energy on deprecating myself and the people who were at the retreat with me. The pettiness of it made me drowsy. It was bizarre: I had come to this paradise hoping for peace, and got the narrowness of my mind's patterns instead.

The longer I meditated, the more I realised how ambivalent my mind is – both gift and curse, depending on how I use it – and this insight liberated me. For the first time in my life, I ceased to automatically associate myself with the things that happened in my head. If my mind had the potential to be an endless source of pain, then why identify myself with it so closely? Instead, I learned to take a step back and view the thoughts inside me from an elevated perspective. It was a revelation: not everything I think, not everything I feel deserves to be taken seriously. I can opt against being taken hostage by what happens inside me, and train my perception and thinking in a way that gives more space for my core.

This was an astonishing discovery, one which brought up new and fundamental questions regarding my own existence. Who am I, if my everyday mind seems to be but one layer of myself? What lies beneath the layer? As I increased my contemplative practice, this question grew and grew inside me. What am I, who am I, once I have peeled away all the things that were never 'me' really, merely mental patterns that I had learned to identify with? Slowly a comprehension dawned. I am both a lot less and a lot more than I had learned to be. More, because there is a whole dimension of my self – my core – beyond the everyday of my learned self, and the mental patterns it comes with. Less, because the core that makes me unique – this essence of myself – constitutes far less: far fewer thoughts, words and actions than my learned self.

To catch a glimpse of this silent, deepest part of myself during my meditation practice, I had to explore unknown territories of my mind. I had to let go of mental patterns I had cultivated for decades. It went against everything my learned self knew. Accordingly, my learned self did its best to keep me bound within the known realm of everyday thinking. This is what I experienced in the meditation retreat I mentioned above. The planning and remembering and bickering my mind was busy with was my learned self's resistance against entering the unknown. Despite this inner resistance, I continued practising. I knew – another example of core knowledge sending out its signals – that this exploration of the unknown would be worth it. Through thousands upon thousands of silent mental cycles, I began to perceive ever more clearly through and beyond my mind's everyday patterns. By accepting these loops, I slowly perceived how my learned mind itself works, just as I caught valuable inklings of my core self. Silently, I discovered new inner territories, so subtle that they had lain undiscovered for decades.

In addition to this, I began to learn to see myself as part of a context that is far bigger than myself. Meditation made me feel the reality of my mortality, indeed the impermanence of all humanity. For the first time in my life I felt a connection to the metaphysical – the eternity of the universe, the great miracle of life, the complexity and beauty of our interdependence. Today, this is a perspective I try to use as permanent guidance, helping me to avoid becoming absorbed in everyday noise which, from a higher perspective, lacks meaning and relevance.

As meditation reminds us, unlearning is an ongoing process. Regression is part of the experience. When I meditate, patterns from my earlier life constantly reach out for me, always grasping to pull me back into the old. Anger, impatience and sadness remain my tormentors. Yet I am in the process of constantly learning to accept them, and see them as what they are. They are fractals of a past that will never be fully over. More often than not, this *seeing* enables me to gain perspective, and to refocus on what matters.

Lever 3: values and purpose – orientating the learned self

Working with the body and the mind is something that happens through immediate experience, not cognitive thinking. It is a practice. For people whose sense of their core is not yet well refined, working with these two levers can be daunting, as they actively threaten the boundaries of the learned self. This is why, as the third lever for transformation, we will look at the fruitful work that can be done on personal purpose and values. In practice, this is more cerebral than the two practices above, and therefore has a 'safer' feel to it: the perfect gateway drug to individual transformation.

Reflecting on individual purpose and values helps us orientate towards what is truly important for us. It can be done by everyone, including people who have no experience with inner work at all, with great and immediate benefits. Within a couple of hours, significant and guiding insights about one's inner sense of direction may be found. These findings may not be ultimate truths (in fact, it is wise to think that any and all answers are provisional and open to reformulation) but the questioning process itself is sufficient to engage self-reflection, bringing our fundamental priorities into focus.

Our values are the unique set of things we find most important, that exert a pull on the decisions we make through our life and as such help us explain why we are the person we have become. Different kinds of values help us gain a sense of orientation in everyday life. The model of the values tree illustrates different levels of values.

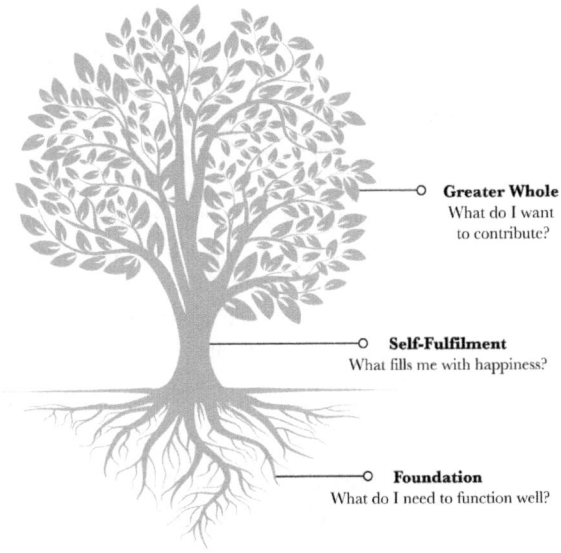

Figure 2 Values Tree (source: SelfLeaders/Unlearn)

First, there are the tree's roots – this is our foundation. Here are found the values which tell us about what we need in order to function and be healthy. Second, there is the tree's trunk, which holds the values of self-fulfilment. These are the keys to what will enable us to have a happy and productive everyday life. The third cluster, the tree's canopy, describes our relationship to the greater whole. These are the values that transcend our individual interests and point towards the greater contribution we aim for, the legacy we want to leave behind.

Choosing your own values can be done quickly and intuitively. Something I've learned is that when you offer people a sample of values, their gut quickly tells them which ones are theirs. I encourage them to choose without too much reflection, and only then do I ask them to consciously reflect on why they chose them: which scenes from your life can help you explain why this value is important to you?

For most people, talking about their values in such a way is a revelation. Accessing and telling their life's stories, they reflect on themselves and what is important to them. Soon enough, people automatically begin to reflect on their everyday environments and actions, and how well aligned these are to the values they have picked out. Significant gaps between what they value and how they live are suddenly cast into light.

Through such values work, people see themselves in a wider context. They see their past, assess the present and connect to the future. They develop a refined understanding of the layers of their self – which values are learned, and thus interchangeable; which ones resonate more deeply with the core. This insight is one reason why values work often leads towards processes of deeper individual transformation.

Values work only gets us so far before raising new questions. We find answers to the question: *why am I how I am?* Pretty soon we hit up against the question that lies beyond it, which values work has no answer for: *why do I exist? What am I here for?*

This is where *purpose work* comes in. It calls on us to reflect on our reason for being. Doing so helps us perceive what we invest our finite life's energy into, and sharpens our sense of the things we can let go of, which fall outside the purpose we defined. Thinking about our reason for existing – and thus our greater contribution – helps us to be less distracted by things that do not really matter, and to divert our life's energy more wisely.

The model I like to use for purpose work is known as the Ikigai. Its structure invites you to approach your reason for being from different angles: what you're good at (or want to be good at); what you love to do; what the world needs; what you are paid for (or want to be paid for). The final part is to consider the greater whole ('what the world needs'), and thus nudges us to reach beyond our individual needs and desires.

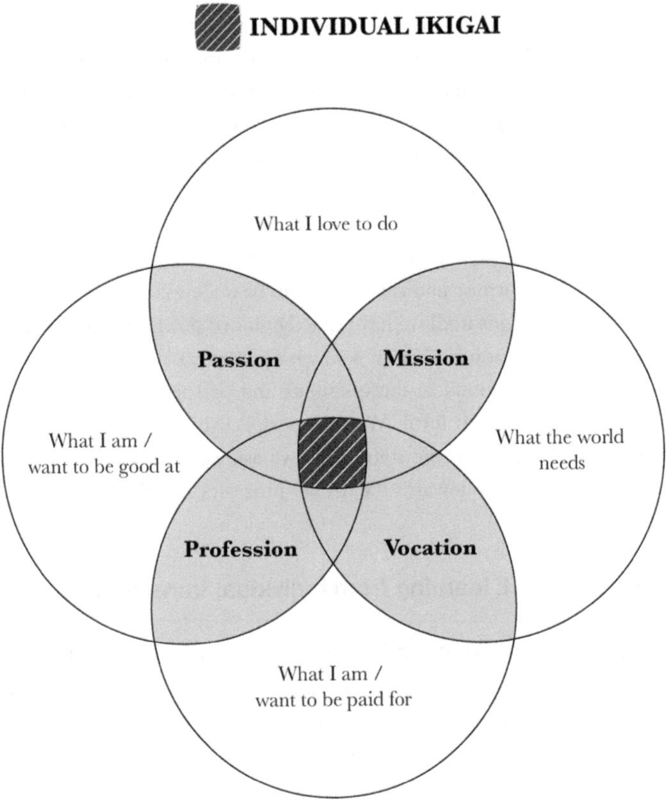

Figure 3 Individual Ikigai
Modified Ikigai model. Source: https://commons.wikimedia.org/wiki/File:Ikigai-EN.svgCreative Commons License: CC BY-SA 4.0: https://creativecommons.org/licenses/by-sa/4.0/deed.en

Doing the Ikigai is easy yet substantial. You start by collecting terms that come to your mind for each of the four circles around the centre circle. Once you run out of thoughts in each of the four fields, you start focusing on the overlaps between the circles. This prompts reflection on your mission, passion, vocation and profession, laying the foundation for a purpose that spans like a roof over these four pillars.

The Ikigai reminds us that there are conflicting dimensions in life, dimensions we have to balance. Our profession should overlap with our passion, but only in rare cases might it be one and the same thing. Our mission may be our inner battle cry, but that does not necessarily get us far towards making a living. And so forth. Formulating a purpose that runs like a golden thread through all these dimensions helps us to locate the common denominator, the guiding star in all aspects of our purpose.

Though often less demanding and intense than body and mind work, working on our purpose and values is not to be underestimated. Usually, it takes many iterations until we have exactly pinned down the purpose and values that truly resonate. Yet, in a way, what matters is not a final result. The true worth is found in the questions and perspectives that purpose and values work brings forth. We shift perspective; we reflect from new viewpoints. We question the status quo; we ask what truly matters. It's a small but decisive step towards the deeper processes of unlearning.

Towards Part II: learning from individual transformation

Unlearning on a physical and mental level, working with our values and purpose; these are some levers we can use to catalyse transformation of the self. By expanding the perspective beyond the learned, these practices help us refine the sense of our core. They support us in taking stock: to acknowledge the person we have become, and to consciously choose which parts of our learned self we might leave behind. The transformation of the learned self thus means the unmaking of our identity. This is a radically creative process. By unlearning, we sever bad lifelines and cultivate new ones.

Our individual journey of transformation calls on us to take responsibility: for the quality and contribution of our own lives, and for the patterns we perpetuate in the environments we live in. By transforming individually, not only do we decide who we aim to be, but also what world we want to live in. In the last chapter, we touched upon how, as individuals, we are fractals of our environment. We mirror what is around us, and what is around us mirrors ourselves. Being aware of this interdependence is crucial. It reminds us that our individual life is not the end in itself; that we can, by meaningfully unmaking and reconfiguring ourselves, further the meaningful unmaking and reconfiguration of the world we are part of.

The transformation of the self also holds several lessons about the transformation of other complex systems. By embracing the realisation that we are a fractal of the systems we are part of, we accept that we cannot transform these systems without transforming ourselves. Secondly, by experiencing the non-linear dynamic of individual transformation, we understand that transformation in other complex systems – for example, an organisation, a community or society – can be neither planned nor controlled. While we can shape our actions to influence this intricate dynamic, we can never say what the result will be, or when it will happen. Thirdly, the transformation of ourselves reminds us what a deeply human undertaking unlearning is. Any human being is a highly complex system. Transforming these systems takes, without fail, constant curiosity, warmth and patience.

We will keep these learnings in mind when, in the next two parts of this book, we discuss the transformation of social systems that transcend the individual: first organisations and finally societies. We will see how the transformation of these systems relies on both individual and collective unlearning. As a fractal of greater patterns, individual unlearning is both the driver and product of transformation beyond the individual.

Part II
Organisational Transformation

Part II

4 The Shadows of the Past

How we limit organisations, and us in them
(the patterns that hold us down – ii)

A COUPLE OF years ago, I was called in to help a team of HR specialists within a German corporation. Their aim was to self-organise as a team, which also meant working without a team lead. To my surprise, the team had a list with very specific questions they were eager to discuss from the very start of the process. One was this: how can we make sure that our disciplinary measures, like issuing warning letters, cutting bonuses or firing someone, will be upheld? Who has the authority to control and discipline in a self-managing team, once the traditional boss is gone?

When they asked me this, I was puzzled. The team's boss had at this point been gone for only a few weeks. No team members had said anything about a lack of discipline being an issue for the team's performance. Quite the opposite. Things were going just fine, without a boss at the levers of command and control. Yet it seemed as if the newly self-managing team could not wait to reinstate measures that, when used, guarantee some of the most degrading moments in professional life.

As I came to understand during our first workshops, parts of the team were guided by the conviction that adults need surveillance and disciplining in order to do their work. I probed this idea with a few questions, and it did not take long to discover that the long list of potential sanctions was hardly ever used. And when it was, what followed wasn't improved collaboration or a better atmosphere within the team, but the opposite. Whenever their boss punished colleagues, mood and motivation cratered. This was an important insight for my clients. They realised how the measures they wanted to reinstate would make them feel humiliated, infantilised.

To me, the team's desire to stay shackled reflected a norm that can be found in too many organisations: adults who willingly reinforce structures of control and discipline which keep them bound in a childlike position, always frightened of punishment or failure; citizens who, when they cross the threshold of their place of employment, willingly submit to despotic leaders, shy away from speaking their minds, and comply with harmful rules and policies.

Why do people accept these destructive norms in the world of work – norms which limit both our individual and collective potential? Understanding this is of fundamental importance when we think about the transformation not just of organisations themselves, but of society. After all, organisations are fractals of the societies they sit within. Their norms both reflect and influence collective norms, and the ways we as individuals operate within society as a whole. To act as levers for positive societal transformation, organisations must establish a different kind of culture on the inside, as a fundament for creating a lasting, positive footprint in the outside world.

The industrial defaults of organisations

Most of us spend much of our waking lives as members of organisations. If this seems entirely normal, in fact it is a very recent historical phenomenon. Only since industrialisation – in Europe, from roughly the 1760s – has the concept of work been broadly understood as selling our time in order to fulfil tasks within a larger organisation that we may be part of, but which does not belong to us. Before industrialisation, powerful organisations of different kinds – the state, the church, the military – were certainly part of daily life. But only since mass industrialisation swept through the Western world have organisations that are centred on the *organisation of labour* become omnipresent and all-pervasive for almost every adult member of our society.

Only since the industrial era have we automatically come to think of the pyramid model of hierarchy whenever we think of organisations: the closer to the top you are, the more power you have; the further towards the bottom, the more powerless. There are those who decide what shall be done, and those who enact these decisions. We accept that work is measured in time we spend in the workplace, and that blue-collar and white-collar work are valued differently. As industrial society created this collective understanding of organisations, so too it established the notion that private organisations exist to produce profit, channelled overwhelmingly to those who own it or work at its top. This society established that organisations belong to those who founded them (or their heirs), not those who work in them. It defined how organisations can use whatever resources they need – natural or human – with minimal conditions other than being able to pay for it; that the only limit on how much an organisation produces is the so-called demand of the market.

This set of beliefs is so widely accepted that they feel entirely natural to most of us. Though they profoundly – and, all too often, negatively – shape the lives of billions of people around the globe, they go unquestioned. We rarely stop to acknowledge that all this is the result of a specific ideology, and a specific political and economic interest at a specific moment in Western history.

Changing the default norms in organisations would, without question, change our lives. Imagine we were at liberty to newly design founding principles and values of the typical organisation. What would we come up with? Do you think we would design an organisation like the industrial one discussed above? Or would we come up with something that works differently? What if society was characterised by organisations – both public and private – which aim to positively contribute to the greater whole? What if they understood themselves as spaces for human development? What if they followed a principle that says: common good trumps profit? This may seem overtly idealistic. Yet our notion that such principles are utopian shows how far we have normalised organisational norms and values with harmful consequences for ourselves and society.

In my eyes, two cultural constructs are most responsible for propping up this status quo. First, we culturally conceive of work as something which is alienating. As a consequence, we accept organisational defaults that limit both our daily joy and impact – after all, we have learned to expect nothing more. Second, by applying different values and standards in our private and our professional lives, we accept professional environments that are unfree, meaningless and disconnected from both ourselves and the greater whole. We devote our days to organisations that wreak destruction on the outside and the inside – results we would never accept, let alone actively further in our role as 'private' individuals.

The reality we see: the cultural preconception of work as alienating

Today's world of work is characterised by an interesting synchronicity. In the Western world, the nature of most jobs has improved massively over the last decades. More and more positions are knowledge-based, characterised by a high need for human creativity and the willingness to accept individual ownership for what one does. The traditional, routine-centred manual jobs of the industrialised world are dwindling – while those that require the development of personal strengths, and thus presuppose a high degree of individualisation, flourish. Yet as the character of work changes rapidly, our cultural attitude towards it lags behind. The way we think and talk about work, the way we carry ourselves in it, continues to mirror the sense of alienation which, for many decades, was the norm in the industrialised Western world. People continue to believe that the rift between the professional and private self is inevitable.

I vividly remember how I felt in my first two jobs after finishing university. At the end of my university years, I worked for a faction in the German Parliament and then moved on to a party headquarters. In both positions, I was given work that was creative and, on a content level, interesting. At the same time, I was confronted with structures, processes and cultures that felt deeply wrong. As a rank-and-file employee, I wasn't allowed to decide anything. Not even my boss could decide – sometimes up to four people had to sign off a single idea before we were allowed to implement it. I had to be at the office for eight hours, even if there was no work to do. Above all, it was apparent that there was no alignment between organisational purpose and daily action. In organisations ostensibly devoted to creating value for society, I witnessed structures and processes that ran counter to this goal. Yet while I disliked all this, I was convinced that what I experienced was normal. I was so steeped in negative presuppositions about work life that I took for granted things which today I see as bizarre and destructive.

Indeed, it was one of my basic assumptions that the *real life* would happen outside of the workplace. This, of course, is a very harmful perspective. By cultivating the idea that meaningful things are done outside of the office, we abandon the expectation that we might use our organisational role as a lever to create something of true value. *Being free*, we learn, is found in *not being part*. Not being part is the prerequisite for doing something meaningful. Self-determination, and thus the active pursuit of aligning the everyday self with the core self, is reserved for those who leave organisations, not for those who stay.

It is thus not surprising that our world is full of stories of people who 'break free' from organisations and establish lives that are truer to themselves outside of the established organisational world. Our culture talks approvingly of senior professionals who exchange their suits for jeans and T-shirt, funnel their resources into good causes, or, freed from the need to earn, start lone-wolf niche businesses. They talk about stepping off the treadmill, about being their own master, about finally doing something meaningful, about giving back to society. When you think about it, the way we celebrate these examples speaks volumes about how far away we are from a reality where value-based, authentic lives in meaningful organisations are the norm. Idolising the few who do break the mould ultimately reinforces the notion that passivity and meaninglessness are what we should consider normal. By singling out people who finally face their responsibility towards themselves and this world, we stress their deviance. It seems we live in a status quo which accepts deep irresponsibility as normal – the irresponsibility of giving away our lifetime for organisations that keep us from feeling a sense of deep meaning, and from creating impact and change that nurtures the well-being inside and around us.

Externalising meaning to the private life

Accepting alienating work as normal is not the only cultural pillar supporting today's status quo in organisations. The second is the stark separation of our lives into the private and the professional.

By signing a job contract, people implicitly agree to a broad array of tacit understandings that are not listed in any legal papers, but that are still considered normal in most organisations: to adapt to the employer's identity and culture, even if you find parts of it uncomfortable. To stick to company policy and team routines, even if they do not make much sense. To respect formal hierarchy, even if it mostly produces confusion and systemic irresponsibility. And, most importantly, to limit your presence, activity and development to the aspects your professional role requires, and to leave the rest at home.

This subjugation to unwritten expectations has functional aspects to it. When you adapt to an organisation in such a way, you facilitate its smooth running, no matter how meaningful its objectives actually are. By accepting its written and unwritten rules, you demonstrate that you aim to belong – and you add to the leadership's illusion that the dynamics within the organisations can be steered and controlled. Furthermore, by bringing only parts of yourself to the workplace, you keep those aspects of your personality at bay that may transgress the boundaries of everyday professional interaction.

At the same time, the subjugation to unwritten expectations often leads to situations that are counterproductive to all sides. Bending to policies you find ridiculous, to serve a boss you do not like and whose values you do not share, in a company whose existence is of no deeper meaning to you – all these things are everyday reality for millions of people. Obviously, this hurts their quality of life. At the same time, their organisation gets hurt as well: the enormous untapped potential of its members is never realised. And, most importantly, society and the greater whole get hurt, by the permanent restriction of our potential – individual and organisational – to dramatically less than it could be.

Using our energy for the greater good

Distinguishing the authentic self from who we are at the workplace corresponds with a very specific understanding of how we enact our individual freedom. When we say freedom, we mean the freedom to establish a private niche where we can live as we want; a freedom from external pressures and constraints. This definition of freedom operates from a reverse, negative perspective. Freedom is then experienced as the place that is *not* work – this moment of relief when you leave the office, when you are on holiday, when you are retired.

Most people feel that their private life is a place of freedom; a place where they can be who they are, without bending their personality, their values and their behaviour to fulfil other people's needs. In contrast, work, for most people, is the place where freedom is a rare commodity. Self-limitation is part of the deal. A fair boss, a stable working environment and a fair salary to most people is the best to be hoped for.

Yet true freedom – reinterpreted to mean a life where we have the ability to develop our consciousness and our capabilities in alignment with core knowledge – is what we need in order to flourish, individually and collectively. When we accept prolonged situations of unfreedom, we nurture the dissonance between core self and learned self. The core self yearns for a free place to *be*. The learned self knows how to satisfy the expectations of others.

Instinctively, when you go to a space that is unfree, you protect yourself. This is what most people habitually do in the professional world. They disguise themselves, to make sure that their vulnerable core is not visible to those in the professional world who have the power to hurt them. When giving talks on the future of the workplace, I refer to the professional mask people put on every morning, before entering the office. Most people relate to this image with depressing ease. They know that mask – a mask that veils your true face and displays what people expect to see: compliance, politeness, only positive emotions, eagerness, motivation... The result of wearing the mask is interchangeability: 'I am like the others – I fit in' is the message.

A couple of years ago, I spoke before 300 senior managers at a large car company. From the stage, I surveyed a mass of dark blue suits, a single outfit differentiated only by ties in different colours. Everyone looked the same. I talked about how the future workplace relies on more authenticity and individuality – while in front of me sat hundreds of people who apparently tried their best to *not* express any such thing. I wondered if they themselves remembered this: that each and every one of them was a treasure, each with an individual blend of personal traits, talents, potential and experiences.

Wearing the mask comes at a deep cost, both individually and collectively. Let us look at the individual level first. Imagine someone who every morning puts on a professional mask that enables her to live values and attitudes that significantly differ from what that person stands for in her private life. She has to cross a wide rift every day, the distance that exists between the self she feels she is, and the professional self she chooses to become. The energy required to bridge that distance each day is lost, swallowed in the void beneath the bridge that spans our private and professional worlds. By putting on the mask of inauthentic professionalism, morning by morning, she robs herself of energy and joy, of the potential of authentic fulfilment and of belonging to the bigger whole.

The collective cost is the systemic consequence of many individual decisions to wear the professional mask. Those who cross a wide rift between private and professional self every day significantly reduce their capacity to create positive impact in their wider environment. They expend all the energy they have just to make it through the day, and then the next, and then the next. Every person who decides not to live her values, not to pursue a higher purpose, takes away energy not only from her individual life, but also from the greater whole.

Towards meaningful organisations

The few examples given here certainly do not cover all the pathologies of today's organisational parameters. They are meant only to cast a light on what we live with every day, but so often struggle to perceive. Most importantly of all, they serve to remind us that the status quo is not permanent and immutable, as it often seems. This is the reality we created as society, reflecting a particular time and environment. It didn't have to be this way, and above all, as with anything we create, we can undo it and replace it with something else.

As we will discuss in the following two chapters, the challenge lies in unlearning these organisational patterns – to acknowledge them and their limitations and to let go of those parts that keep us from creating purposeful everyday realities. If we do so, we can harness the enormous power and potential of today's organisations: as levers for the transformation of society and the world we live in.

5 Unfolding Human Uniqueness
Towards cultures of self-authorship
(sensing the new – ii)

WHEN WE look at the world of work today, we are beginning to see the principles of an emerging organisational model. A kind of organisation that establishes structures and cultures that are closer to the needs of employees and of society. In exploring the features of this new model, in the mid and long term, the whole economy will see a shift towards this emerging model as the old, industrial model increasingly fails to meet the needs of our times. The implications go far beyond the fate of single organisations, or even sections of our economy. Such a shift has the potential to be no less than a driver of societal transformation.

In many ways, we are at a decisive moment – a moment in history when we have the opportunity to renegotiate what organisations should be there for, and what work should look like. The emergence of this new type of organisation is driven by external developments that are putting the industrial organisational paradigm under tremendous pressure. There are three main drivers that force organisations to transform, and to unlearn their old models. Firstly, digitisation and automation. Secondly, rising complexity. Thirdly, an unstable political and social environment making a narrow focus on profit, rather than purpose, unsustainable. Let us look at these in turn.

Organisations for the digital age

The world of work is – today and in the coming years and decades – subject to profound structural change. Digitisation disrupts all sectors of society. Automation and artificial intelligence are altering work as we know it. Experts disagree on the exact degree to which these developments will impact our everyday working lives. But they are unanimous that massive changes in the entire economy will continue, in one way or another.

For many decades, automation has been a threat predominantly to blue-collar workers who did routine manual labour. Today, advances in artificial intelligence technology means routine cognitive tasks can be automated as well. Humans are being replaced by machines with ever-increasing speed. Already, corporations lower the number of administrative professionals they train, as they expect significantly reduced need for human resources due to more sophisticated software.

At the same time, artificial intelligence promises to replace not just routine work, but also to reduce the need for professionals who do more sophisticated and varied mental work. Analysts, lawyers, bankers, tax consultants, insurance experts and many more are expected to be forced to fundamentally change the way they work in the next decades. These professions will – and, in many cases, already do – face intense competition from automated versions of themselves.

This, of course, has far-reaching implications for how organisations work. Think of a company you know from the inside – what would the hallways look like if all those people who do routine-centred jobs today (think especially of logistics, administrative or legal departments) were missing? What would happen when those workers, who historically are used to highly formalised environments with top-down leadership, are all but eliminated by waves of automation? How would the everyday culture change once the majority of remaining workers are those doing creative, non-routine work – work that relies on their unique personal talents, competencies and potential?

As we saw in the last chapter, humans have the capacity to adapt to organisations. Within the industrial work paradigm, they fit themselves into the narrow, rectangular boxes of the organisational chart. Now, in the era of automation and AI, this dynamic may be reversed. Suddenly, humans face the task of doing work that is individualised and highly creative, to set themselves apart from what machines can deliver. In this world, the development of individual potential, the cultivation of the attitudes and skills we need for co-creation, the unfolding of diversity becomes a must. The successful organisations of the future will be those that harness both the widely available power of technology *and* the unique power of flourishing individuals. While machines and artificial intelligence can, at least theoretically, be replicated by competitors, people, by contrast, are unique. They are what creates difference, and they are what will help organisations be creative, innovative and likeable.

It cannot be stressed enough how radically this will change the way we work. For modern capitalism, the substitutability of individuals was the key success factor. Modern organisations, mostly focused on mass production, thrived because they made themselves independent from the individuals who constituted them. They reduced them to repetitive manual tasks. And when one person became sick, demotivated or too expensive, companies could replace them with someone else who then fulfilled the tasks of the job description. In the coming years, at least in certain segments of the job market, this principle will be done away with. While the need for workers in general may decrease, there will be a rising need for top talent. As in the tech sector today, highly skilled workers will go where they can be who they are, and where they can choose autonomously how and at which pace they want to develop themselves. As a consequence, organisations must be built around the radical unfolding of human uniqueness.

The power of lateral leadership: self-organisation as response to complexity

Today's focus on the digital revolution means we often forget that, even prior to the digital era, the economies of the developed world were undergoing massive structural change. By the end of the 20th century, globalisation had radically changed market dynamics, and thus how successful organisations operated. Economies that once were national are today part of an immensely complex, worldwide market.

During the Covid-19 crisis, we tangibly felt how intensely intertwined the globalised economy has become. Once the markets in China or India shut down, the Western world realised how much it relied on these countries for producing even the most essential goods, like medicine. And indeed, while the global population has been interconnected via trade for centuries, the degree of international economic interconnectedness today is unprecedented. As a result, we feel crises in countries that are thousands of kilometres away only days – sometimes just hours – later.

These dynamics of globalisation create an intricate, infinitely complex web of interdependencies no one fully understands. As we know from systems theory, complex webs like the modern global economy have some fascinating characteristics. For instance, the more complex a system, the higher its volatility. This means that pace and intensity of sudden change increases with rising complexity. This increase does not happen in a linear pattern, but exponentially. To make matters worse, one can never reliably tell where these sudden changes originate – or, to look at it another way, which outcomes one's own actions will cause in other parts of the complex web.

Today's widespread acceptance that stability is a thing of the past results from this effect. We simply observe the chaotic symptoms of the global economy's complexity. A further consequence of this is a rising incapability to predict what will happen, even in the near future. One can analyse and calculate and so make an informed guess – but coming even close to certainty is impossible, no matter how refined one's prognoses are. As a result, most organisations suffer from profound disorientation. In the past, almost every company had an overall strategy, which in turn was broken down into targets and plans for the organisation's different parts. Today, this kind of long-term planning has become impossible.

As a growing number of organisations realise, the capability to swiftly and smartly respond to an ever-changing environment has become far more important than the capability to plan and project. Not surprisingly, agility has become a buzzword over the past few years. Frequent, iterative planning and decentralised adjustment to reality as it is (instead of as it has been planned) is a strategic asset in times when planning becomes close to impossible.

Another symptom of the rise in complexity is the specialisation of roles in organisations. When the structure of the market becomes more and more complex, an organisation needs a lot of specialised knowledge to develop its products, to be able to communicate with its stakeholders, to analyse shifting market needs, to keep up to date with innovations in one's field, and so on. As a response to that situation, organisations differentiate on the inside, and thus mirror parts of the market's complexity. Naturally therefore, it has become harder and harder for managers – even team leads – to understand what their people work on, and thus to make a decision in their field of expertise. When I talk to people in senior management positions today, most readily admit that it is next to impossible for them to understand what their team members do much of the time, simply because the breadth and depth of knowledge they would need to do so exceeds the capabilities of one human being.

This is why, today, great bosses are those who enable their teams to lead themselves, and to eliminate problems they face. In the future, this will be a must. As computers and machines will be ever more intertwined with professional roles, the breadth of complex interactions one person must comprehend will increase further. In such an environment, the structural, professional, and personal ability to act and decide autonomously is key for successfully responding quickly to real emerging demands. The success of an organisation thus relies on the capability of each of its employees to autonomously decide and act however she – according to her expertise – sees fit.

This insight chimes perfectly with findings in systems theory. The more autonomously a system's parts can respond to changes in the (outside or inside) environment, the quicker the system as a whole adapts. If, on the other hand, a system's parts have to wait for a central authority to permit their response, the capability to successfully adapt decreases dramatically. A decentralised culture and a high degree of self-organisation thus are key for an organisation's ability to successfully navigate in complex environments.

Purpose: creating legitimacy and orientation in a contested environment

Complexity, automation and artificial intelligence are on the agenda of most organisations today. More and more leaders understand that their ability to navigate in this environment decides their organisation's fate.

Simultaneously, another question demands increasing attention. The ongoing climate crisis exerts pressure on all organisations. For instance, as I write this chapter, millions of young adults take to the streets every Friday to demand swift political action against climate change. These demonstrations are a symptom of the deep unease that has accumulated over decades: we cannot continue to live the way we have lived during recent decades. Our model of living, producing and consuming is not normal; it is excessive. In response to the resulting pressure, more and more businesses begin to reflect in earnest: how can we better align with the needs of society and the ecosystem?

Obviously, sustainability and corporate responsibility are not new issues. But, arguably, this is the first time there is serious public and political pressure to truly deal with these issues. For many years now, organisations have learned to pretend to have a cause that transcends profit as sole purpose. The web is full of marketing statements that, supposedly, explain how companies accept social and ecological responsibility. But, as many of these companies will readily admit once off the record, most of these statements lack sincerity and have had no serious consequences for the overall business model, however destructive it may be.

Today, the quest for a meaningful organisational purpose and sustainable business models has become a question of existential importance for an increasing number of companies. In times of fundamental self-doubt and rising public and political pressure, defining a purpose that explains an organisation's contribution to the greater whole is of high strategic relevance, on the one hand, in terms of explaining public and political stakeholders what an organisation's overall contribution to society is; and on the other, in orienting the organisation itself towards an overarching goal in times of transformation.

As rising complexity makes it hard to predict the times ahead, a genuine and meaningful purpose helps to strategically orientate an organisation in times of uncertainty. An organisation's purpose may not spell out how to successfully navigate uncertain terrain. But it increases the overall sense of orientation by enabling employees to bring into focus their employer's overall reason for existence, and the greater contribution their organisation is striving for. If taken seriously, this helps to sharpen the sense of the general direction one should take, which in turn makes it easier to align day-to-day strategic and tactical decisions.

Importantly, a meaningful purpose creates a strategic lifeline for organisations in a shifting political environment. I believe it is certain that we will witness a renaissance of politics over the coming years, with radical reforms that reshape the fundament of entire markets (see Part III). This will likely be accompanied by rising public scrutiny with regards to the negative cost-externalisation of business models. In such an environment, organisations who follow a purpose that feeds into the greater whole will be under severely less strategic pressure than those who continue to be exclusively profit driven.

We will discuss the transformative power of organisational purpose in more detail later, as one lever for initiating transformation in organisations. The important point for us now is that a meaningful purpose reshapes how we organise organisations. If taken seriously, structure, process and culture are oriented towards it – which is a major lever for rethinking and rebuilding structures and processes.

The emerging organisational model: five core principles

Taken together, the developments we discussed in this chapter make the transformation of the industrial organisation towards a different model a strategic necessity. The individual, economic *and* societal perspectives call for a new way of doing things. The question, of course, is: what should an organisation look like to meet the needs of society, the market and its employees?

The honest response to that is: nobody really knows. We have not found a 'new normal' yet. The whole organisational world is in a state of fundamental transition. Yet when we consider the trends we discussed above and look at the experiments with new organisational models that are already underway, certain core principles of an emerging organisational paradigm can be perceived. I summarise these in five points. Each is a response to today's individual, economic and societal needs – and each marks a significant shift away from the paradigms and patterns we discussed in the last chapter.

Principle 1: Structures and processes are derived from organisational purpose and values

Developments in the outside world are now too complex, too ambiguous and too volatile to provide a reliable basis for setting a mid- and long-term course. In a world that feels increasingly unstable, and in markets that are constantly and rapidly changing, organisations that are able to cultivate a sense of orientation from the inside are those that navigate successfully. A shared purpose and organisational values strategically align the organisation, and enable individuals and collectives to act coherently. Ideally, purpose and values constitute the gravitational core of an organisation. Structures and processes are like layers that are grown around them, evolving constantly across all levels.

Principle 2: Formal hierarchies lose relevance

As we discussed in the last chapter, when we think of organisations, we have learned to picture a pyramid-shaped organisational chart. This industrial model often suffers from slow decision-making due to clogged bottlenecks, and infighting between internal silos. Antithetical to this, a growing number of organisations have opted to abandon formal, permanent hierarchy, instead opting for a more self-organised, decentralised structure. In these organisations, autocratic decision-making power is based on competence, granted as a privilege – and can be revoked.

Principle 3: Leadership is distributed on many shoulders

As a consequence, the nature of leadership changes fundamentally. Gone are the days when there was one centralised decision-making authority. Instead, leadership is decentralised. People who fill certain roles accept decision-making authority within their professional domain of responsibility. The bottom line is that every role is expected to be 'self-managing' and thus carries a lot more responsibility than most employees would within a traditional pyramid hierarchy.

Principle 4: Cross-functional and cross-hierarchical collaboration defines the organisation

When structure and leadership become decentralised, it is harder for departmental silos to permanently establish and entrench themselves. In the emerging organisation, the external or internal need defines which roles and teams it takes to fulfil it. Project teams and coordinating circles come together in a fluid way, and are driven by the need to include all relevant perspectives. Collaboration across functions and hierarchies thus becomes the norm.

Principle 5: New ideas trump the status quo

When structure, leadership and collaboration are in constant flux, the organisation as a whole is highly fluid. While traditional organisations see phases of change as the exception, in the new paradigm, constant evolution is the default state. This has far-reaching consequences, especially for the pace of internal innovation. In the industrial model, innovation is the exception: 'You need great arguments and political acumen to change the status quo.' In the emerging model, this is replaced by 'You need very good arguments to *stop* a good idea from being piloted.' As a result, a culture of prototyping evolves: to quickly try out new ideas, instead of endlessly debating its pros and cons. Once prototyped, an idea can always be improved or replaced if the results are not what people hoped for.

Taken together, these five principles sketch out an organisation that is highly adaptive to changes in its environment *and* internally. This is an organisation whose default state is fluid, more self-organised and more decentralised than what we are used to, where individuals at all hierarchy levels hold the power to initiate change – a radical shift compared to the industrial organisation, where a dynamic of lateral powerlessness is systemically enforced.

Being driven by a common purpose, being self-organised and structurally empowered turns the industrial culture of detachment and alienation on its head. In this context, wearing the mask of professionalism we described in Chapter 4 is not only unnecessary, it is counterproductive. What the emerging organisation strives for is congruence between person and organisation. It relies on individuals who opt for being present. The core question this organisation asks is fundamentally human: *how can you, by living your individual purpose and values, further the purpose and values of our organisation?*

The transformative challenge: establishing cultures of self-authorship

As we discussed in Chapter 4, today's status quo supports the industrial organisation and its paradigms and defaults from the past. The entire legal and regulatory environment incentivises the cultivation of industrial organisations. Indeed, organisations that aim for a new operating system often feel that today's laws and regulations force them to maintain industrial principles they would like to replace with more sensible ones.

This is mirrored in the entire set-up of today's institutions. We are very far from systemically enabling individuals – be it in kindergarten, school, university or professional training – to fill responsible, self-organised roles at the workplace. Yet the developments we have discussed in this chapter build up pressure to transform. What we are living through today are the early stages of a deep paradigm shift. While most organisations – including the biggest and most powerful – still act from the industrial paradigms and defaults, there is a tangible movement towards the emerging organisational model. Many organisations have begun to experiment with the five core principles we discussed above.

As more and more organisations feel the pressure to abandon the failing industrial model of doing things, they wonder: how can we successfully master the transition from the industrial to the emerging organisation? As they quickly realise, a culture of purpose and self-organisation cannot be implemented or bought by an external service provider. What it takes is the careful cultivation of something new from the inside.

To understand this point better, let us go back to Robert Kegan's model of adult consciousness development, which I introduced in Chapter 1. Taking individual transformation as example, we focused on the challenging but crucial shift from a socialised level of consciousness to a self-authoring one. As we saw, only a third of adults act from a level of self-authorship. The majority (around 60 per cent) operate from a socialised mindset. This consciousness level is focused on pleasing others, fulfilling externally defined expectations and abiding by rules. The socialised mindset enables individuals to fit in and to please higher authority. It drives us towards fulfilling existing norms and rules, no matter if they make sense to us or not. Individuals who operate from a socialised paradigm are able to function in environments where their values and needs are not met, be it by pretending, adapting or disappearing; this is the destructive understanding of professionalism we discussed in Chapter 4.

By contrast, self-authoring individuals are capable of aligning their behaviour with their inner compass, instead of being fixated on one that is externally defined. While they know how to fit into social systems – which they learned during their socialised phase – their higher purpose and values, when in doubt, trump the needs and wants of their peer group. Accordingly, self-authoring individuals have a higher sense of inner guidance. When in doubt, they have a general sense of orientation, due to the higher purpose and values they defined for themselves. This enables them to autonomously plot out the path forward, even when there is no map that shows them the way.

Kegan's model lends itself to considering not only individual levels of consciousness, but also the collective consciousness of organisations. It helps to understand which level of consciousness is ingrained in an organisation's structures, principles, processes, policies and unwritten culture. This, then, helps us to understand why certain attitudes and behaviours evoke severe conflicts in one organisation, while they are perfectly normal and accepted in another. Also, the concept of self-authorship reminds us that it takes a certain stage of individual consciousness to realise self-authorship on a collective, organisational level.

As we sketched out above, industrial organisations by default expect their employees to follow orders. These organisations are based on an authoritarian mindset, one that places the burden of all decision-making on a privileged few, while most members of the organisation are expected to do as they are told. They want their staff to be compliant, which also means, when in doubt, to refrain from making decisions and instead ask the hierarchical superior. If we look at this model through the perspective of Kegan's five stages of consciousness, we see that these organisations are built around an imperial and socialised mindset. These organisations expect people to behave along the lines of authoritarian praise and punishment, to fulfil requirements defined by others, no questions asked.

In contrast, when we consider the five core principles of the emerging organisational model, we quickly realise that they cannot be brought to life by individuals who operate from an imperial or socialised level of consciousness. To fill the emerging model with life, organisations need individuals who are able to operate from a stable level of self-authorship: people who do not merely do as they are told, but who reflect on why and how they want to do the work they do; people who constantly transcend and redefine the boundaries of their professional actions, who willingly accept responsibility and decision-making power; people who encourage both themselves and others to break the patterns they learned, make mistakes, take risks.

The need for cultivation from the inside

The transformation of an organisation towards a culture of self-authorship thus depends on two main factors. First, an organisation needs principles, structures and processes that incentivise autonomous decision-making and the orientation towards a higher purpose and shared values. Second, it needs individuals who are capable of filling and re-interpreting that space, thus creating a living culture of self-authorship.

To successfully initiate and nurture a transformed organisation, you always need both ends of the deal. Implementing self-authoring principles and structures will end in chaos and frustration if you lack the people who are able to use the space you create with it. If, on the other hand, you put socialised individuals into structures that require self-authorship, then resistance, frustration and, at times, chaos will break out. This is simply logical: people who rely on rules and regulations to feel safe do not blossom from one moment to the next when you push them into spaces that require their autonomous initiative and decision-making. What these individuals need are safe spaces for personal development, to slowly push their mindset's boundaries towards the next level.

At the same time, hiring mature individuals who operate from a self-authoring mindset will change little to nothing if you keep organisational structures and processes in place that incentivise imperial or socialised behaviour. Organisations that try this usually hope that the self-authoring newcomers will leverage the culture to a new level. But recruiting new faces alone does not transform an organisation's DNA. What happens instead is that self-authoring newcomers regress to imperial and socialised behaviour when they enter industrial organisations that incentivise those levels of consciousness. Or, more frequently, these people leave sooner than expected because they do not feel the organisation offers them the environment they need to be motivated and happy.

There is no quick fix, in other words. Organisations that aim for a self-authoring culture must cultivate new structures, processes and mindsets from the inside. As we will discuss in the next chapter, this is hard – but it can be done.

6 The Seeds of Transformation
Levers for organisational unlearning
(levers towards the new – ii)

ORGANISATIONS ARE instruments to bring into this world something which single individuals could not achieve. Their contribution to the greater whole is what constitutes their reason for being. Transformation is the process that improves the organisation's capability to contribute meaningfully. Unlearning the paradigms and defaults from the past is merely a key requirement for defining more productive ones.

In this chapter, we will look at three central levers for cultivating the seeds of transformation, levers which help to open spaces for individual and collective unlearning. They facilitate self-authoring environments, and help overcome the sense of alienation and soullessness discussed in Chapter 4.

First, we look at how dialogue on purpose and values is vital for successful transformation. Second, we discuss how the individual transformation of leaders helps to initiate organisational dynamics towards self-authorship. Third, we learn how the cultivation of spaces for genuine human encounter facilitates and deepens the development of a self-authoring culture.

Lever 1: purpose and values

Cultivating a self-authoring environment in an organisation calls for a dissemination and democratisation of leadership. Transformation asks for the entire organisation to unlearn, and collectively create a new, better reality. We will discuss below how working on an organisation's purpose and values helps to catalyse collective unlearning. To better understand why purpose and values are so vital, though, let us take a moment and look at the differences between individual and organisational transformation.

When an organisation transforms, its development is both driven by and is a driver of the dynamics between the people who 'make' the organisation. People will react to the changes around them in ways no one can predict in advance – which then, again, triggers new dynamics that no one can foresee. This interdependence makes the transformation of an organisation far more complex than its individual counterpart.

The individual journey is about *gaining and refining* our sense of the core self, and aligning with it. By contrast, organisational transformation is about consciously *re-creating* its purpose, and collectively aligning culture, structure and processes with it. As we know from companies with decades-long histories (like IBM, for instance), organisations have the potential to redefine their entire reason for being, and with it the paradigms and culture they foster on the inside.

Like individuals, organisations are bound by the paradigms and patterns they developed in the past. The culture of an organisation – its learned self – is the product of that past, including its structure, processes, policies, norms, behaviours. Just like at the individual level, unlearning these

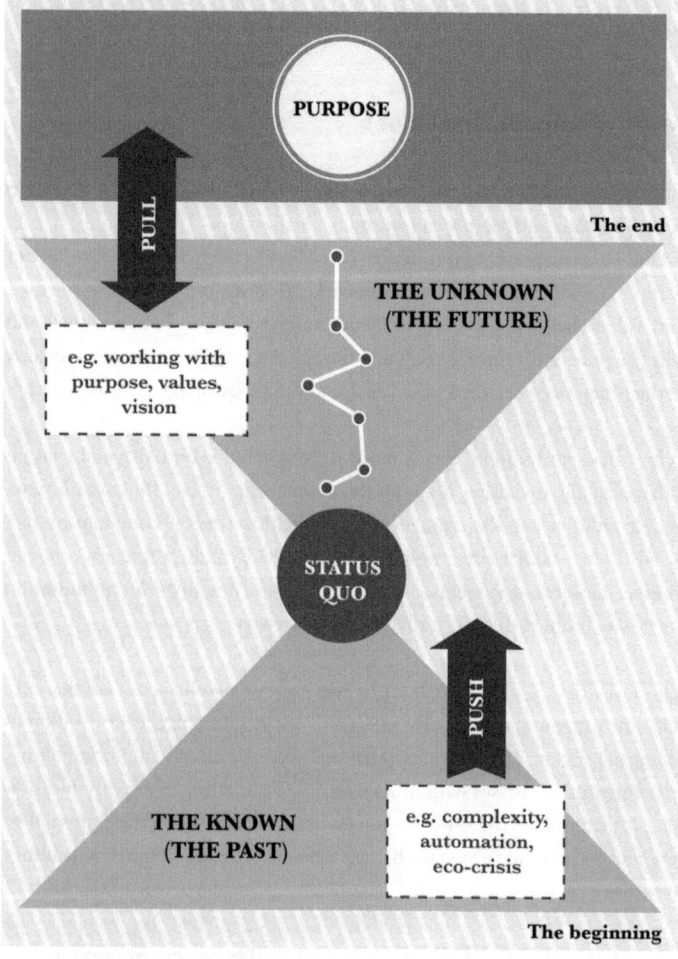

Figure 4 Organisational Transformation

patterns takes an acknowledgement and letting go of parts of one's learned identity, thus entering the unknown.

As we saw in Part I, individuals are drawn into the unknown by core knowledge, gravitating the self towards its core. For individuals, this core is a given – an intrinsic fact of being human. For organisations, this is not the case. They must consciously define their core self, or purpose. This purpose ideally serves as the gravitational core of the organisation, a core that facilitates a shared sense of meaning, orientation and alignment, especially in times of uncertainty. It helps people to make autonomous decisions which are still aligned with the overall organisational core. It creates a sense of synchronicity in decentralised, self-organised environments. And it serves as a filter between the organisation's outside and inside: people who positively respond to a specific purpose will be more likely to be the right ones, those who join and stay as opposed to those who don't. All this makes the purpose a north star, which is why it should be defined at the start of transformation processes.

One key to organisational transformation thus lies in finding this purpose – and in aligning the organisation's inner workings with it. This process has massive strategic repercussions for how an organisation transforms its structures, processes and culture.

A powerful purpose provides an organisation with its guiding narrative: why do we exist? What is our contribution to the greater whole? It anchors the organisation within the world, and defines the cause it drives forward. It keeps the organisation from becoming self-referential. And it helps people to critically reflect on the premise their organisation stands on: do we positively and sustainably contribute? And what must we do to sustain this? Asking and answering these questions enables an organisation to bring into focus the truly meaningful. Doing so has profound strategic value. It orients the organisation towards expanding its positive ecological and social impact – which is the best investment in its long-term survival.

In Chapter 3, we discussed how the Ikigai helps to refine one's sense of individual purpose. The Ikigai is an excellent model for organisations as well. It integrates the systemic perspective, as it asks what the world needs. This makes organisations take account of the wider context in their purpose work – a strategic must in today's environment.

Co-creating an organisation's Ikigai unveils organisational core knowledge: inklings, feelings, ideas of an alternative reality which, until then, were an untapped resource. The goal is to collectively anchor in the future, to create a shared image that is powerful enough to start unlearning the patterns of today's culture. Ideally, it creates a powerful pull towards something new; a pull that makes it easier to let go of the old.

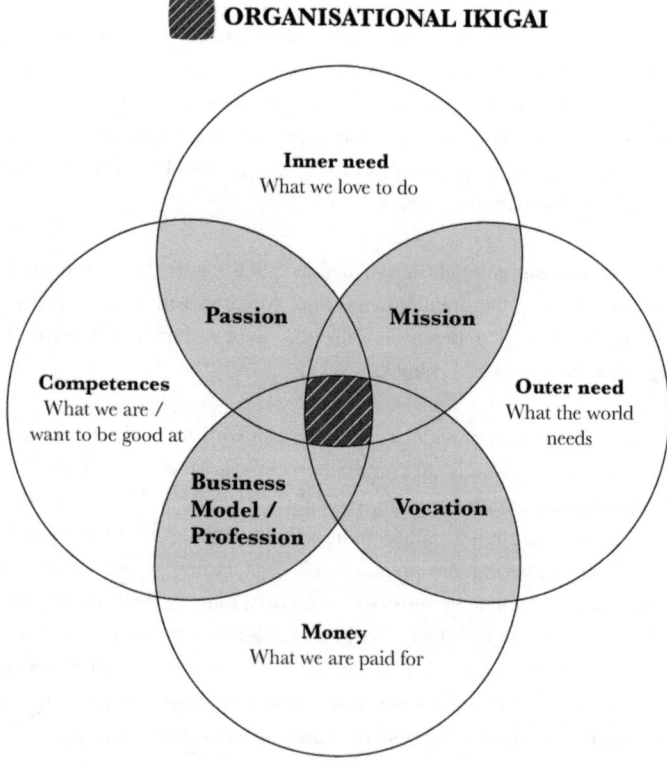

Figure 5 Organisational Ikigai

Modified Ikigai model. Source: https://commons.wikimedia.org/wiki/File:Ikigai-EN.svg Creative Commons License: CC BY-SA 4.0: https://creativecommons.org/licenses/by-sa/4.0/deed.en

This offers a wonderful opportunity for people to experience a self-authoring space. Here, they can feel into what their organisation might become, by exploring different futures and emotionally relating to them. This can have powerful consequences for how individual members of an organisation relate to it, and see themselves in it. The shared creation of an organisational purpose gives them the opportunity to reflect individually on their employer's cause: how does my life's contribution fit into my organisation's purpose? Can I personally relate to this goal – do I feel it is worth investing my time and energy for it? Indeed, a powerful upside of such processes is that they actively counter the sense of alienation and meaninglessness we discussed in Chapter 4.

To make the purpose a tangible force in everyday work life, it is important to translate it into values that both express and catalyse it. The purpose contains an organisation's reason for being. Values, on the other hand, spell out the principles that help fill this purpose with life at the level of everyday collaboration. Values thus operate at the level of how an organisation works, providing a set of principles that help align people in terms of how they support and treat each other.

Values – if filled with life – can be true pillars of a purposeful everyday culture, and help pull the organisation towards the future it desires. Ultimately, they are constant reminders and active servants of an organisation's purpose. Yet defining values – just like defining a purpose – does not *per se* have any positive effects on organisational culture. What matters is how they are brought to life, by giving people the opportunity to emotionally relate to them, individually and collectively. Once this happens, an organisation's purpose and values catalyse the integration of private and professional. They nudge people towards being present – and to connect their personal values and ideals with what they do at the workplace. This expansion of self-expression shifts the attitude towards the workplace; it is an antidote to the harmful detachment and alienation that too often hold us down today.

Lever 2: leaders who unlearn

Many leaders understand that their organisation's industrial cultures, structures and processes are a huge liability on the path ahead. Despite this insight, they have a hard time finding a meaningful role in overcoming this status quo. The mindset they cultivated in their career hinders them from living the transformation they publicly proclaim. I have witnessed how entire organisations remained stuck in the status quo because of their leaders' inability to transcend their individual patterns. Cognitively, they may have embraced the idea of organisational and personal transformation – but by behaving in the way they behaved, by believing what they believed, by thinking the way they thought, they prevented deeper transformation from happening. By not developing *themselves*, they severely limited and sometimes existentially threatened the success of their organisations.

Yet the more profound the transformation, the more willing leaders must be to unlearn individual patterns that keep them stuck in the status quo, and with them their entire organisation. They are the ones who must *live* the transformation they want their organisation to master. In doing so, they can be role models for everyone within the organisation, a highly visible fractal of the transformation everyone is part of.

I remember an entrepreneur who had grown what was a small family business in southwest Germany into an international organisation with over a thousand employees. Driven by his initiative, the company went through a process of transformation that aimed at strengthening self-organisation, individual responsibility and decentrality. This process was initiated by the owner's insight that the command and control leadership style he had learned in his earlier life did not deliver what the organisation needed. The owner felt that, in order to continue to grow and stay successful as a company, he needed to break with the common wisdom of what an organisation looks like.

After initiating a multi-year transformational process, it took five years before a shared sense of ownership and a higher degree of lateral leadership had rooted in his teams. As he told me, this process of adaptation was slowed down by himself. For a few years after the start of the company transformation, he was unable to personally follow through with what he demanded from his employees. As a consequence, he realised, he had to change as an individual: unlearning his patterns, his values, his leadership style. This, he said, took time. At the same time, he soon realised that whenever he managed to let go of one pattern, this created positive ripple effects for the whole organisation.

This is important to keep in mind. When we say organisational transformation, we talk about a process in which people, individually and collectively, unlearn how they perceive, think and behave, with profound implications for how they organise their collaboration and the interaction with the outside world. The deeper the transformation must go, the more prepared the participants need to be for situations that feel uncomfortable, insecure and sometimes frighteningly unstable (compare Chapter 1).

You may realise how such processes go fundamentally against the default behaviours most managers cultivate while climbing the career ladder in their organisation. Especially in corporate structures, they succeed by planning and controlling, and avoiding uncertainty by any means. Which explains why initiating transformation is so hard for them. So what can be done to help leaders overcome their psychological resistance, built up over a whole career?

One lever is to prompt leaders to reflect on their experience with transformation beyond the professional. This has three upsides. First, tapping into personal histories of transformation makes leaders reflect on the non-linear, unplannable nature of transformation. This is a powerful nudge to call into question the traditional plan-and-control approach to traditional change programmes. Second, by reflecting on their own life, leaders open up emotionally and relate to their organisation's transformation on a level that goes deeper than the functional and rational. Third, personal histories of transformation make people understand that they have specific transformation experiences they can build on. This helps to gain a sense of confidence and orientation – and thus build a fundament for leadership – in times of distress and uncertainty.

Let us start with the last point. I often talk to leaders who tell me they do not know how to approach the transformation that lies ahead of them. When these people tell me that they do not have the experience it takes to tackle transformation, I challenge that notion. Once people dissolve the mental boundary between private and professional, they quickly acknowledge that they, actually, have profound and directly relevant transformation experience: times when not-knowing and not-controlling was a fundamental prerequisite for developing towards a better place; when they chose the dreadful uncertainty of transformation over the fragile certainty of the status quo. Once people take that perspective, they realise that individual experiences of unlearning and transforming can be very helpful for initiating transformation at an organisational level.

For instance, I once worked with a CEO who was about to launch a transformation programme for his entire organisation. He felt helpless. In his eyes, he lacked the experience for such a profound process. When we started expanding the perspective beyond his professional life, he quickly realised that he was wrong. As he told me, he was deeply shaped by his experiences as a young East-Berliner after the fall of the Wall. In the first months after German Reunification, he said, everything he had learned about politics, the economy and the state, had to be unlearned to be able to navigate the new system. In everyday life, his entire community was in complete disarray. He, his family and almost everyone around him were confronted with existential uncertainty. As the CEO realised, this phase during the early 1990s was a valuable resource for the transformation he was about to initiate. After all, he mastered the difficulties during those months and years, gaining experiences that deeply shaped his personality. Acknowledging these 'private' biographical resources gave the CEO confidence for the transformation he would initiate in his organisation.

This story helps to understand the other upside of connecting with individual histories of transformation. By reflecting on his individual journey, the CEO quickly understood that the transformation of his organisation would take time, and moments of disorientation and pain – just like his transformation did. That it would result in a new learned self he could not yet know. He understood that, while overall goals of development could be formulated ahead of the process, mapping out the exact road towards these goals would be futile.

By taking his individual story as reference point, his thoughts about his organisation's process were anchored emotionally. Instead of thinking about the transformation of his company in abstract terms, the CEO was closely connected to the ups and downs of his own journey. He clearly felt the aliveness of the process that would follow – the human quality of it. When he communicated his core ideas to his employees, this emotional openness enabled his colleagues also to connect on an emotional level. This gave the process depth from the start; a crucial factor for a dialogue that fosters trust, commitment and quality.

Lever 3: collective unlearning in safe spaces

Shared dialogues on purpose and values can serve as catalysers for processes of transformation. But they are not enough. To anchor individual and collective processes of unlearning in everyday life, more and deeper spaces are required. Spaces where people can reflect, individually and collectively, on the patterns that hold them back, and openly exchange their experiences and learnings. This requires formats that lie beyond achievement, where genuine human encounter is possible – and open dialogue and new behaviours can establish themselves.

Intimate spaces of dialogue are key for catalysing and deepening transformation. Once experienced and enjoyed, they create ripple effects which change the permanent quality of how people relate to and work with each other. They substantiate transformation, because they make the process spiral from the level of words and ideas to the level of feelings and the sense of being touched by those around you. One small moment can create a reference point for everything that follows. These spaces are not an end in themselves. They create the safety and mindfulness it requires to become aware of patterns that limit collective transformation. Also, and just as importantly, they create an environment where others can be made aware of how they behave.

As I learned over the years, the challenge lies in creating dialogue spaces that are both safe and intimate. You may notice that both words are rather unusual in professional contexts. Safety requires the acknowledgement that most professional spaces are unsafe – we justifiably fear being attacked and hurt. And intimacy is a word we usually associate with our private lives: with moments when we open up, moments that show us in our vulnerability and imperfection. This breaks with how we have learned to behave in professional environments. We carefully select which parts of ourselves to show to our colleagues, and what to keep unseen. In a way, we hide our core, instead of using it as a steady point of orientation for who we are and what we choose to stand for, privately *and* professionally. Transformative dialogue spaces aim to replace this pattern with shared settings that are open yet safe.

A while ago, I worked with a small consultancy company. Their vision was to transform towards a culture of self-organisation and, as part of this process, a new ownership model that distributed shares among all team members. But once the team members got the opportunity to buy, no one did. We set up a dialogue to dive into this finding: why such a difference between vision and reality? It quickly became clear that, while everyone still wanted their company's transformation, the trust needed to realise this vision was lacking. As we unearthed, the team saw their boss as the main obstacle on the way forward. They described him as hierarchical and, at times, aggressive. When we dived deeper into this, the owner shared how hurt he was by the team's perspective. He asked why the team had not told him earlier. As he realised during the course of the conversation, due to his tendency to react aggressively when someone criticised him, no one had felt able to confront him about it. This had left him with the impression that the team was fine with his leadership style and enabled him to maintain the self-image he had.

The owner was only one side of the coin, of course. When we explored why the team had such a problem with their boss's behaviour, we found out that several team members had a history of bad professional experiences. It became clear that they had experienced their former bosses as a daily threat to their well-being and had learned to be cautious and defensive in the workplace. As the team understood in the course of our conversation, such histories made them react very strongly towards the owner's behavioural patterns.

As disappointing as this dialogue may have been for the team, it was highly important for the company's further transformation. The team had connected on an emotional level and increased their understanding of how they saw each other, and which obstacles would need to be eliminated before driving the company's transformation further. Indeed, after this conversation, the company revised and adapted their plan and came up with ideas that were more fitting to their constellation and culture. Mapping out this new path was made possible by the trust created in the dialogue above – a fundament for unlearning, both individually and collectively.

What this example shows is how transformation depends on situations that make issues speakable which usually remain in the shadows of the unsaid. This may be uncomfortable, but it is vital for transformation to be more than a cognitive idea. These are the moments that make everyone understand that things are really changing (or, in the example above, why they are not). Such openness, and the intimacy that comes with it, is key to paving the way for development beyond surface changes. It is a prerequisite for a transformation that goes beyond what the leadership wants, what an industry or cultural trend says, or what the market demands. A transformation born from within, emerging from the core of those who drive it.

Towards Part III: transformed organisations as levers for transforming society

The way an organisation transforms always mirrors its individuals' state of consciousness. Individual stories of transformation can initiate processes of fundamental change in the entire organisation. At the same time, fundamental changes in an organisation have deep repercussions for how individuals grow and develop. Ultimately, this interdependence between the individual and collective levels is what makes or breaks the transformation of an organisation. If organisations managed to structure themselves around self-authoring purpose and values, this would have tremendous ripple effects for how we organise as society. This way, people could get used to a default where they are led by an overarching purpose, not the short-term satisfaction of material goals.

Organisations that transform make their members understand that human-made systems can be changed. During the process of transformation, people feel – both individually and collectively – that their attitudes and actions make a difference. As we will discuss in the next part, this experience is something we urgently need in a world that is stuck in the belief that the status quo cannot be changed. This is why, right now, organisations should be regarded as an experiment laboratory for changing the defaults, particularly in terms of how we organise collaboration. If we manage to transform our daily lives in organisations in accordance with self-authoring principles, this will enable us to approach central societal issues like personal and collective development, leadership and self-leadership, and deliberate self-organisation in a more meaningful way – with, potentially, many fruitful mirror effects for how we organise ourselves as a civilisation within the ecosystem.

Organisations that transform have the potential to serve as fractals of societal transformation. Their learned patterns mirror society as a whole. If they manage to unlearn these patterns, and replace them with new ones, this has repercussions for the whole of society. After all, these examples create stories that show it is possible to do things differently. And if this can be done at an organisational level, why should it not be possible to do something similar at the level of a community, or society as a whole?

Part III

Societal Transformation

7 The Pain We Cause

Confronting the destructive society (the patterns that hold us down – iii)

To live a full life, individuals need a sense of purpose. Bringing the learned self and core self in close alignment can unleash tremendous amounts of positive energy: a flow that enables us to work towards what generates good in this world. On a physical level this flow must end with death. Yet the ripple effects of our lifetime's actions keep on spreading after we are gone from this world. This is how our individual lives make a difference – fractals of transformation that can further the meaningful development of the whole.

Organisations, just like individuals, have the potential to create something meaningful when guided by a positive purpose and values that are realised on an everyday level. They enable people to collectively create a whole greater than the sum of its parts. When transforming, organisations have the potential to be experimental spaces, establishing mindsets and practices that encapsulate stories and learnings for the transformation of society.

Now, how can we use the insights from looking at individual and organisational transformation when we look at the transformation of society? As we will see in the following three chapters, societal transformation follows a logic comparable to the one we encountered in the first two parts: first, the acknowledgement of the learned self, in all its ambivalence; second, the imagining of a better reality, and the definition of a purpose that serves the future instead of the destructive status quo; and, finally, the unlearning of patterns that hinder us from moving towards the unknown.

Though the logic may be the same, societal transformation is far more complex than transformation at individual and organisational levels. This is due to society's complexity, as well as how it is subtly intertwined with those levels we discussed in Parts I and II. In a nutshell, there can be no societal transformation without the transformation of its individual and organisational fractals. At the same time, intentional steps of transformation on the societal level exert a profound influence on how its parts – individuals and organisations alike – themselves develop. The transformation of society thus is both driver and result of individual and organisational transformation.

This dynamic, in its enormous complexity, is hard to grasp, both emotionally and intellectually. Yet it is vital that we understand it better. Many of the frames Western societies created over the last several decades are crumbling: our economy, our political institutions, our sense of who we are in this world. More importantly, the fundamental frame that holds these frames is itself teetering. The ecosystem that holds all of us is acutely suffering from mankind's sustained violations of its boundaries. It is of utmost urgency to face the question of what it will take to meaningfully transform society. And, more importantly, which society we aim to create by transforming it.

This is the existential question of our time: how can we shape society in a way that unleashes its positive, creative potential, instead of its violent, destructive one? How can we create new, more meaningful paradigms for our societies and economies – paradigms that are more sustainable and empathetic than those dominant today?

In this chapter, we will start by looking at the patterns that hold us down collectively – patterns that keep us stuck in *this* reality: ground rules, mental models and (mis)perceptions of what is 'normal'; explicit and implicit parameters that keep us from transforming, even though, on a cognitive level, we all know that we cannot continue to live the way we do today. We will touch upon three crises we face: the socio-ecological crisis, the democratic crisis and the spiritual crisis. Crises which are symptoms of the destructive defaults our societies are built upon. Crises which therefore cannot be solved through any changes we might make within the given parameters, but require us to unlearn, reimagine and realise new ground rules for society as a whole.

The following two chapters will introduce ways in which we might collectively imagine a more meaningful society, a different kind of politics and economy. In other words, this part of the book is not about how we 'fix' things. Many excellent books will tell you which measures we can take today to systemically tackle the multifold crisis we are in. Instead, Part III focuses on how we can develop a clearer sense of a shared future. A future that draws meaning from the purpose to reintegrate ourselves within the ecological and social boundaries of this planet and global society. A future that, properly imagined and shared, can draw us towards the transformative steps we need to master in order to realise it.

1. The socio-ecological crisis

For some years now, scientists have spoken of the Anthropocene, the age where humans shape the ecosystem more than any other force on this planet. From taking up more and more land to the drastic reduction of the variety of plants and animals to the impact our emissions have on the climate: humans have altered the delicate balance supporting all life on this planet, with changes that cannot be undone.

We are familiar with this story: over the last 150 years, humans have created a global abundance of material wealth. The industrialised economy has enabled the enormous material enrichment of Western economies from the 18th century onwards, and the rapid material development of non-Western societies from the 20th century. Improvements in living conditions and life expectancy have made the global population explode. Extraordinary social accomplishments have accompanied this rise in material wealth. The major threats to human civilisation for its entire history – namely, famines, plagues, scarcity – do exist today, but at a very reduced level. At the same time, individual rights and freedoms have made leaps forward, not only in Western democracies but also in the vast majority of societies. Overall, the individual – ever the focus of modern liberal society – is better off than ever before in human history.

While we all know about these positive developments, we are also aware of their negative flipside. Material wealth may have reached an all-time high, and yet it is accompanied by massive inequality. Today, the world's eight richest men own more than the poorer half of the global population. At the same time, there is environmental carnage. Our way of producing and consuming has fundamentally altered the self-regulation of the ecosystem, and the man-made climate crisis is altering the basic properties of the planet's life web.

I can almost hear you saying at this point: 'I've heard all this before.' And I am sure you have, just like me. The remarkable thing about today's crisis is exactly that: that we all know about the catastrophe that is happening, but that we fail to transform towards social and ecological sustainability. Indeed, the very discussion of today's crisis has become boring to our ears. We have cultivated a wilful deafness to what is paramount for the future of human civilisation, and the well-being of this planet. It seems as if the havoc we cause fails to truly touch us beyond the cognitive. We will return to this dissonance later in this chapter. Before that, however, let us look at where in our history these destructive patterns, now playing out on a global scale, are rooted.

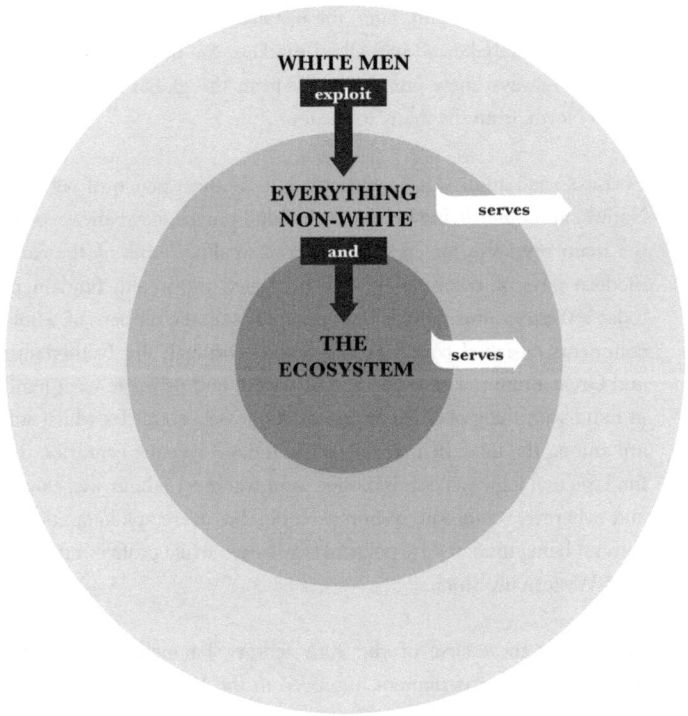

Figure 6 Pre-Modern Model

Our liberty to destroy

For most of their modern history, Western societies didn't care about the degree of environmental and social destruction their way of life caused. For half a millennium now, social and environmental exploitation has been an integral part of the global North's cultural, political and economic DNA. Though the means of this exploitation changed, the basic dynamic has remained the same since the early modern start of the Western capitalist economy. A privileged few benefit massively, externalising the negative cost of their actions to the less privileged, to countries not their own, to other species and to the future. Ever since the imperialist expansions of early modern times, through colonisation and, later, the installation of so-called 'free' yet intentionally unbalanced globalised markets, the flow of capital and resources always knew one direction: from the global South to the global North, from the many to the few.

Cost-externalisation was – and still is – at the essence of all this. Nature, and other living beings, including humans, have always been the main resources for creating material wealth. Think of the early modern days of colonisation, which created the wealth fundament today's Western prosperity is built upon. Systematic robbery of whole continents enriched countries like Spain, Portugal, the Netherlands and Great Britain. The expansion of wealth and privilege went hand in hand with the global expansion of those very countries which still are among the most rich and powerful today. Over the centuries, the fundamental logic persisted: money went wherever labour was cheap, and wherever common resources could be over-exploited, ideally without being hindered by political regulation, while profits went back to its Western investors.

While, over the course of the 20th century, labour conditions and the state of the environment improved in the West, both precarious working conditions and ruthless environmental exploitation were outsourced to other parts of the world. Today, this exploitation of cheap 'foreign' natural resources and human labour is at the core of Western purchasing power. Moreover, cost-externalisation as a basic societal principle is more relevant than ever in the history of humankind, due to its adoption by formerly non-capitalist countries like India and China. What once was the fundament of a small minority of the global population has become the basic logic of global society as a whole.

The logic of cost-externalisation is not a mere economic principle. It shapes our individual and collective self-perception. In the West, this principle has become such an integral part of our collective learned self that we find it hard to imagine a world where limitless cost-externalisation is not part of everyday reality. We feel individually *entitled* to produce and consume solely based on our own decision-making, even if the sum of these 'free' individual decisions violates

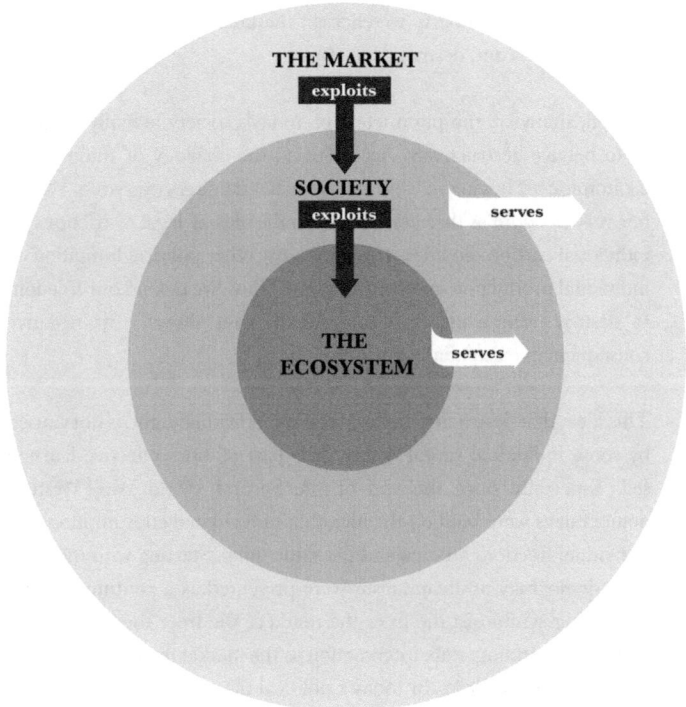

Figure 7 Today's Model

other humans and species, and destructively interferes in the self-regulation of the ecosystem as a whole.

As democratic societies, we have high respect for the *fictional*, man-made boundaries set by societal culture, the constitution or laws. But the *factual* limitations of the ecosystem's resources are continuously violated, as an integral part of our way of life. It is quite astonishing once you think about it. Our cultural, political and legal liberty is limited by various boundaries: explicit ones, like the constitution and laws, and implicit ones like social norms. However, *economically*, our liberty is all but unlimited: there are basically no boundaries at all for both consumption and production. As long as individuals and organisations have the financial means, they are free to do as they please. This is the liberty we cherish: the liberty to destroy. A liberty that, as it turns out, destroys ourselves.

Indeed, many of the parameters of today's society actually *encourage* us to behave destructively. According to the ideology of mainstream economics, *not* buying new products is what damages everyone. We see our very freedom as threatened by even the idea of legal restrictions on individual carbon dioxide emission, or any other political limitation of individual production and consumption. Thus, we defend our freedom to destroy even while – as the climate crisis shows – its negative consequences existentially harm us.

This idea, that destructive behaviour is an individual right, is not caused by some individual moral defect. It is part of our collective learned self. Especially since the end of the Second World War, Western democracies were built on the idea that unregulated consumption and individual freedom are one and the same thing. Starting with the Cold War, democracy and capitalism were presented as a continuous, life-enhancing symbiosis: the freer the markets, the freer the societies. In that understanding, state intervention in the market means the curbing of individual freedom. In today's political discourse in the West, this non sequitur still enjoys near-universal acceptance. As a consequence, we lack alternatives for how to reorganise the market, how to govern consumption, how to rescue as many species as possible, how to organise and coordinate a sustainable global society. Instead, we seek solutions within the existing system, the very one that has caused today's existential crisis. And, yet, there must be an alternative.

In many ways, today's societal situation goes back to what we discussed in Part I: the tendency to prefer the discomforts of the known, even if this status quo brings with it permanent negative stress and pain on a mental and physical level. We hold on to what we know, preferring the sense of orientation within the uncomfortable while avoiding the disorientation that comes with entering new, unknown territories. The unknown may hold a better life for us. Yet our fear of it can be so great that we continue with those patterns that existentially harm us.

This collective paralysis is cemented by political institutions that are unable to broker solutions for the existential challenges we find ourselves in. Nation states created this globalised economy, an economy that has grown so powerful that its creators are unable to govern it according to the common interest. Most states are not in a position to defy those powerful corporations who massively benefit from the current lack of global governance. Major corporate superplayers – the main beneficiaries of globalisation, mostly located in Europe and North America – have revenue streams that exceed those of most nation states (today, the ten biggest corporations have a combined revenue of more than 180 countries).

Overcoming our broken and harmful system will be impossible if we do not acknowledge the limiting patterns that keep us stuck in today's self-destructive status quo. Such patterns define us, and they limit our ability to transform as societies. As long as we fail to acknowledge and unlearn these notions, we will remain paralysed in the face of existential systemic challenges: knowing that we have to change, but unable to imagine how to do so.

2. The democratic crisis

Over the past decades, most democracies failed to tackle the major challenges of our times, namely the climate crisis and the massive levels of national and global inequality. Instead, the West has driven both developments by fervently pursuing an agenda of globalisation and deregulation. As a consequence, the social and political situation in Western societies has changed dramatically over the past 30 years. What, for decades, seemed confined to the global South is in the process of becoming normal in Western democracies. Inequality of wealth and opportunity is at an all-time high, unseen since the 1920s. Instability has taken hold of both the political and economic sphere, going hand in hand with rising degrees of poverty, populism and social unrest. As a consequence, Western democracy looks increasingly fragile. The disparity between the system's ideals and the promises it makes to its people, and the reality it creates, grows ever more visible.

As we increasingly realise, today's economic model not only destabilises the ecosystem as a whole, but also the functioning of democracy. The socio-ecological crisis and the democratic crisis go hand in hand, as it turns out. How have we reached this point? How has the crisis of the economic system turned into a democratic crisis? To understand this better, let us dive a little deeper into the evolution of liberal democracy and market capitalism, and their relationship to each other in the years between the post-war settlement and today.

The forgotten roots of post-war prosperity

Though now they are often conflated, liberal democracy did not always equal a 'liberalised' (i.e. deregulated) market economy. True, most of the 18th, 19th and early 20th centuries were characterised by an uncompromising capitalist paradigm. As we know, environmental destruction and massive social stratification were the result, leading to increasing political instability in the global North through the first half of the 20th century.

In many ways, the polarised social situation we are in today is, from a historical perspective, neither unusual nor exceptional. Our societies have been there before. Yet collective self-perception is strongly shaped by the short, exceptional decades after the Second World War, a period when politics, for a moment, decided to rein in and subjugate the market to the needs of Western society. During that era, Western democracies exhibited a clear understanding that markets are man-made instruments, to be used for creating prosperity for the whole of society. To achieve this potential, the state had to actively define parameters and rules that tempered the inherently anarchic dynamic of capitalism. For the first time in modern history, politics gained the upper hand over economic interests.

The post-war willingness to politically interfere in the market resulted from the pre-war experience of untrammelled laissez-faire capitalism, which resulted in massive social instability. In Germany for example, the crass economic inequality during the 1920s was one of the main drivers of rapid political frustration and radicalisation that ended in the political ascendancy of the Nazi regime. In the United States, an extreme form of capitalism resulted in the formation of a small, super-rich elite while mass destitution shook the country.

What made the post-war political impetus so different? In a nutshell: the Cold War. A competition between worldviews and systems, with the very survival of each system on the line. This drove Western politicians towards avoiding high degrees of inequality and the resulting instability, accepting social measures they never would have previously countenanced. After all, capitalist democracies had to produce evidence that their system was capable of benefiting the whole of society.

We tend to forget from today's perspective, but in the 1950s and 1960s it was far from clear whether socialism or capitalism would win the Cold War. Systems change was a constant possibility, not an abstract thought experiment. It was the political response to this threat which drove the primary cause of the famed post-war boom era. Today's narratives have it that this era came thanks to the magic of an unregulated economy, but the opposite is true: post-war prosperity was a product of massive state intervention in the capitalist market.

Take the United States for example. The state was active everywhere – it actively and successfully distributed wealth to the growing (white) middle class. The redistribution of wealth, on a level unthinkable today, was a major priority for the US government. Accordingly, in the years during and after the Great Depression, the country opted for a highly interventionist approach. Higher incomes were massively taxed: top earners paid up to 94 per cent during the Second World War, and the top tax bracket remained well above 70 per cent until the era of Ronald Reagan. Indeed – and almost forgotten today – by the end of the Second World War, 90 per cent of the prices of everyday goods sold were politically controlled. Such measures enjoyed high public approval, just like the intense state intervention into the education sector and the job market. Such massive political interventions in the economy enabled millions to study, to get cheap credit for buying real estate, and to profit from a booming economy. The success of the famed consumer economy after the Second World War was thus in large part initiated by an interventionist state, focused on improving the welfare of the bottom 50 per cent of incomes. Comparable stories could be told for the whole of Western Europe.

'Free markets for free societies'

It did not take long, though, before a more untamed version of capitalism regained the upper hand. The expansion of individual material wealth quickly became the primary focus of most governments in the West. As a consequence, democracy and politics was increasingly driven towards the expansion of the capitalist market. Over the years, the perception of the economy shifted, from being a signifier for democratic freedom to being an end in itself.

By the late 1970s and accelerating through the 1980s, many Western business leaders, politicians, economists and journalists had become convinced that a free (read: unregulated) market and a free society were one and the same thing, and that there was an automatic, positive interplay between the two. Economic liberalisation and democratic well-being became Siamese twins in the dominant narratives of the Western bloc.

When the Cold War ended, the distinction between capitalism and liberal democracy had become so blurred that introducing democracy as a political system was assumed to be one and the same thing as the radical liberalisation of markets. After the fall of the Berlin Wall, this ideology led to the systematic selling-out of public goods in the former Soviet Union, and a massive redistribution of wealth towards (Western-owned) global corporations and the privileged few. The infamous economic 'shock-therapy' reforms led to the destruction of the material safety net of hundreds of millions, an existential experience of collective disorder and the shattering of bonds of community.

As a result, regions which formerly were characterised by social stability – especially in the former Soviet Union, but also in the Americas – experienced a radical and intentional destruction of societal structures, in the name of liberal democracy. Their experience did not remotely resemble the Western post-war story of rising equality and prosperity. Rather, democracy brought with it years of fighting for survival, a weak state, the colonisation by Western corporations, massive wealth and income inequality and, as a consequence, a deeply divisive societal climate. In these countries, 'liberal democracy' is seen as nothing but a Trojan horse for a radical market economy.

The end of an alliance

At the same time, and despite the increasing economic, social and political turmoil in neighbouring regions, Western Europe and the United States seemed like havens of political and social stability and economic prosperity. Sure, there were countries like Greece, Belgium or Italy that fought with high unemployment rates and high levels of public distrust in the political system. But in general, Western Europe and the US seemed immune to the turbulences that shook the world elsewhere.

As we have seen in recent years, though, the West is not after all immune to the destructive dynamics it heaped on the rest of the globe. The same dynamic of rampant, destructive capitalism that caused severe social and political crises in other parts of the world, has now returned to the capitalist heartlands. With the fall of the Soviet Union, the political will to even contain the violent forces of capitalism ebbed away. As a consequence, Western politics increasingly subjugated itself to the needs of the market, embracing the self-destructive logic that corrodes the very foundations of the societies that created it.

Privatisation, deregulation and the weakening of social safety nets have structurally altered the distribution of wealth in Western countries, and thus basic societal dynamics. The last 30 years brought tremendous amounts of wealth to the upper 20 per cent of society – especially the top 1 per cent – and precious little to the remaining 80 per cent. For the lower half, incomes have stagnated, and at the same time the quality of social safety nets has been significantly reduced. There is growing public awareness that the primacy of the political has been replaced by the primacy of the economic. Over recent years, this was spelled out in brutal clarity for the citizens of countries like Greece, Spain or Portugal, where European institutions and the IMF incentivised the dismantling of basic state structures, riding roughshod over the democratic will of the people in the process, for instance via the installation of unelected 'expert governments'.

What is decisive here is that the weakening of social security and the flexibilisation of the labour market has led to shifts in how significant parts of Western society perceive democracy, as a system and as an idea. For decades, inequality and exploitation through cheap labour was something that happened in distant parts of the world. Now, these phenomena increasingly characterise Western societies. Democracy – the force that once promised inclusion in society and a share in collective prosperity – is now perceived as a threat to individual well-being by many. Distrust in democratic institutions' ability to aptly solve the challenges we face has crept into the very heart of Western societies.

As long as we continue to conflate liberal democracy with liberalised markets, this dynamic will not change. The democratic crisis will continue to worsen as long as we avoid new responses to fundamental questions: what is democracy there for? What must it deliver to be legitimate in the 21st century? And which kind of economy serves this purpose? We will only find meaningful responses to such questions if we acknowledge that many of the patterns we collectively cultivated over the last century or more are not fit for carrying us into a better future. In other words – and we will discuss this in more depth in the next chapter – we must face our collective learned self, in all its ambivalence, to be able to identify and leave behind some of the patterns that hold us down as societies today.

3. The spiritual crisis

The symptoms of the socio-ecological crisis and the democratic crisis are omnipresent as we look around the world of today. Indeed, they look set to reach ever greater heights in the years ahead. How do we respond to finding ourselves in such a situation? Conceivably, we could say: 'We had a blast! We raced through the planet's resources in merely 200 years – and it was great. We enjoyed being the world's aristocracy. We loved our plasma TVs, flying around the world and driving our SUVs. We know we brought the world to the brink of collapse. But we don't care. Because we are hedonists. And because we love our lifestyle so much, we'll just keep going until the shit hits the fan.' This sentiment would, at least, have the virtue of aligning perfectly with our actions. Still, I never heard a single person honestly say it. Though we continue daily to act in this way, there is no sense of joyfulness, or happiness. We may be strongly attached to a lifestyle of cost-externalisation. At the same time, both catalysed and expressed by the crises we discussed above, we realise that today's model has come to an end, and that the ground we stand on is a lot less stable than we used to believe.

There is a spreading sense of a fear that is uncannily silent: an unavoidable awareness of the onrushing consequences of our actions. This fear is all the more potent because it extends beyond our individual destinies. It is rooted in a deeper place, a broader consciousness than the worry about our individual well-being: the consciousness that we are irreparably damaging this world, a world of beauty and perfection that transcends our individual lives in scope, depth and meaning. It is the rising awareness that we lack the power to control what we have unleashed. We fear the shame that comes with this admission: that we, as a privileged elite of humanity, have made and continue to make everything suffer for our privilege.

This truth is there, right now, in every one of us. But often very subtly, like a constant, deep humming: a movement we can constantly and very deeply feel in all parts of our system, an unease that lies far beneath the level of everyday emotion. We all feel it, some with more, some with less consciousness regarding its existence. A humming of guilt and the shame that runs through us, making us constantly feel: this cannot continue.

The more we increase the pressure on the planet, the more pressure we feel within ourselves. The symptoms of this rising tide of dread and unease are everywhere: the rise in public distrust against the political system is one. The booms of cryptocurrencies. The rising number of suicides in industrialised countries. The mental illness epidemic. All these phenomena may seem unconnected at first sight. But ultimately they all are symptoms of rising individual and collective anxiety, fear and distrust. Such indicators help us to understand that the instability and fear we subtly feel individually is actually something collective. Something in our shared consciousness is shifting. Beyond all divides that characterise our societies, we are united in an existential feeling of dread.

Western society is in a deep spiritual crisis, a crisis that silently encompasses us. This spiritual crisis springs forth from the ever-present, subtle awareness that we cannot go on like this. Instead of acknowledging it, we devote our energy towards blocking it out. To be able to continue with the havoc we cause, and to be able to ignore the suffering we unleash, we collectively silence what goes on inside.

This massive, taxing internal resistance is what produces the disconnect we repeatedly touched upon earlier in this chapter; a disconnect that enables us to endlessly talk about the climate crisis, environmental destruction and structural inequality, without actually tackling the patterns that cause them. A disconnect that enables us to continuously focus on the satisfaction of individual self-interest, while the world around us burns. The detachment from what we know is true brings with it a detachment from ourselves. We feel disconnected from the greater whole we are part of, we long for reintegration – yet we can't achieve it while we are stuck within the patterns that hold us down.

Tapping into the shared sense of unease

The discomfort we feel on a subtle, spiritual level is nothing more or less than core knowledge, as we discussed in Part I, manifested at a collective, societal level: an expression of existential discomfort that pushes us towards considering alternatives to the patterns of the learned self; a deep kind of knowledge that sends us signals from inner realms beneath the cognitive.

We discussed in Chapter 1 how core knowledge sometimes forces us to change direction, by sending signals from a deep self we may have been out of touch with. It is a force that expresses itself in signals of discomfort – signals that nudge us towards acknowledging and unlearning those patterns that go against our core. It is individual, inner experience on a most existential level, using our entire system to make us understand that we must change direction.

The emerging of core knowledge, while experienced and expressed individually, is the collective, metaphysical response to these destructive patterns of the collective learned self. It is pushing us towards exploring the unknown, and towards letting go of harmful patterns that we learned to see as 'us'. We will discuss in the following chapters how, by actually leaning in to this shared sense of unease, we can start societal conversations which may enable us to realise that there is an alternative to the status quo. The first step towards such a conversation is the acknowledgement that we are each full of existential dread. This humming emotion, however uncomfortable it may be, has the potential to be the major impulse towards rediscovering our ability to create meaning collectively, and to discover alternatives to how we constitute reality today. Our fear can help us to confront the disastrous heritage we and our ancestors created. It can bolster our willingness to accept short-term disadvantages for long-term gains. It may spark the crucial shift of our everyday perspective: from an overriding focus on our individual, egoistic needs towards a more careful consideration of what our environment and global society may need, and how we can contribute to it.

8 From Paralysis To Transformative Purpose
Towards future society (sensing the new – iii)

I**N THE** previous chapter we sketched out the trifold crisis we face: the socio-ecological crisis, the democratic crisis and the spiritual crisis. We discussed the subtle yet existential dread we feel regarding the course of global society, knowing that today's model is not viable, while, at the same time, feeling stuck within it.

In this chapter, we will explore what it takes to develop a sense of the new, and thus overcome this collective state of paralysis. We will take two perspectives. First, we will look at society's urgent need for a new purpose that offers orientation during the era of transformation that lies ahead. Second, we will discuss the two main pillars that societal transformation is built on: the political realisation of reforms on the one hand, and bottom-up self-organisation on the other.

Expanding perspective: asking fundamental questions

In the first and second part of this book, we learned how vital it is for both individuals and organisations to refine their sense of their core: that a different future, a different reality is actually possible. An idea of what a better future could look and feel like is crucial for developing the motivation to let go of the known, and to unlearn limiting patterns of the learned self. While individuals can autonomously refine the sense of their core, and derive a sense of purpose and direction from it, organisational transformation takes the collective development of a shared idea of the future. This process has repercussions for the development of individuals who 'make' the organisation: single parts of the social system who, by changing individually, generate transformative impulses for the organisation as a whole.

In many ways, societal transformation mirrors these dynamics, on a larger and far more complex scale. Like organisations, societies need an understanding of what holds them together: most importantly, shared values and thus principles of living together. And, also like organisations, societies require a shared sense of purpose and direction, especially when their environment changes – the sense that something positive lies ahead, that the transformation of society is guided by a higher idea, instead of being nothing but the defensive reaction to a changing world. Most Western societies today lack these factors. There is no shared idea, no shared desire of where society could be headed. The only thing people feel is a growing, deeply disquieting sense of discomfort, resulting from the insight that society must change course.

As we discussed in Part I, core knowledge can express itself in signals that cause deep discomfort – signals that make us realise we must unlearn. On the societal level, a comparable dynamic takes place: as the frame we live in crumbles, we feel the boundaries of what is thinkable and speakable fall away. The growing collective discomfort drives us towards questioning the status quo. Yet our collective capability to explore possible futures is severely limited by various factors. First, as we explored in the last chapter, we are deeply shaped by learned ideological beliefs regarding capitalism and democracy. The firmness of these patterns keeps us stuck in this reality, severely limiting the perspective on possible futures. Second, we respond to today's crisis with frantic attempts to apply fixes to the status quo. The measures we take are scattergun, incremental and often contradictory, but they absorb great amounts of energy all the same, and thus distract us from finding more substantial, systemic approaches to today's challenges. Third, we are unwilling to stop and acknowledge our fundamental cluelessness regarding how we can get out of the mess we created over recent decades and centuries.

Once we stop and reflect, we quickly understand that we lack answers to the most basic strategic questions regarding our society's course, questions we must find responses to if we want to develop a sense of purpose and direction. What do our societies exist for? What is their positive contribution to today's and tomorrow's world? Where do we see ourselves in 10, 30, 50 years? And which kind of political and economic system derives from the responses to these questions?

What do democratic societies exist for?

Let us take a closer look at the first question: what do today's democratic societies exist for? What, from the perspective of today's and tomorrow's challenges, is their higher reason for existence? Once you start thinking about this, you will realise that today's Western societies lack a sense of purpose. They have lost their understanding of what they exist for, and thus have no sense of direction and orientation. Along with this confusion has come decreasing alignment regarding what 'democracy' actually means.

In Western societies, 'democracy' is part of our everyday vocabulary. We speak of democracy as if there is such a thing – but democracy is, first and foremost, an idea, an ideal, a hope. This idea has morphed quite extensively over time, to an extent that makes it hard to speak of 'an' idea; it has been a myriad of ideas put into very different practices over the course of centuries, and around the globe. The meaning of democracy is fluid, and its meaning has always been and will always be contested. This also goes for Western democracies today. There is less and less alignment regarding what is 'democratic'. Indeed, there are more and more political players – especially on the populist right – who, quite successfully, maintain that today's representative democratic systems are actually *undemocratic*. They present them as rigged against the majority of the people, as it is representatives, not citizens, who make political decisions. These political forces, just like reading history books, remind us that democracy can mean many different things. Democracy *can* mean the tyranny of a voting majority. It *can* mean a direct-democratic rule within constitutional boundaries. It *can* mean the idea of representative democracy. Indeed, 'democracy' can mean many things – which makes it even more important to consciously decide *what we want it to be*.

In its original sense, democracy signifies nothing but the rule of the majority. This definition, though, is not what has come to define the core of Western democracies today. Most countries around the globe accept majority-based elections as a principle, yet quite clearly not all of these we would consider truly 'democratic'. It is certainly possible to act in accordance with the majority principle while actively undermining the rule of law and individual freedom rights. Potentially, minorities can be exterminated with democratic majority approval. One can be democratic – in this sense – *and* trample minority rights. There can be rule of law without democracy; there can be democracy without the rule of law.

What we today refer to as 'liberal democracy' is a governmental system that bases its decision-making on a legislative majority that is limited both in time and powers. We mean a system with a constitution, and structural checks and balances that limit the degree of executive power and protect individual and collective freedom rights. We mean the rule of law, the protection of minorities… and yet, a list of such characteristics merely describes *how* we organise democracy. It does not tell us what the *purpose* of this democracy is.

I believe that this is where the paralysis of today's conversation on democracy and its future comes from. The proponents of democracy confuse the structures and instruments of the democratic system with its purpose. They feel profound unease when one questions the current ground rules of the political system, of how we organise representation, or of how we structure and organise elections. This unease stems from a lack of differentiation: what is the *core* of democracy we should protect and thus not transform, and what are *instruments* that are meant to serve the well-being of a democratic society, and thus should be subject to constant questioning and improvement? Arguably, parts of this state of confusion go back to the intentional blurring of lines between democratic purpose and democratic instruments – the neoliberal dogma of the equivalence of 'free' (unregulated) markets and 'free' democratic citizens (see Chapter 7).

The future potential of democracy: towards a new democratic purpose

Whoever cares about the future of democracy must therefore distinguish between its structures and instruments and its purpose. Looking back through the history books from the first interpretation of democracy onwards, we see how, in modern times, democracy has always been focused on the individual, geared to facilitate its citizens' liberty and happiness. The liberty that democracy grants to its people to grow and develop freely is what distinguishes it from autocratic regimes, who aim to limit the development and self-expression of their citizens. Yet this focus on the individual falls short, as long as it is based on an understanding of liberty that focuses on the immediate satisfaction of material needs.

What we do not find in history books are examples of democracies that rest their identity on a truly systemic perspective. While we may understand what democracy has to offer for individuals, we do not yet grasp what it has in store for the well-being of the overarching systems we are part of – either the ecosystem or global society. Yet today's crises show us clearly that democracy *must* take this bigger whole into account. It can only last if it enables its citizens to develop a consciousness that takes into consideration not only the well-being of individuals, families and communities, but also the overarching systems that hold these entities, from overall society to nature as a whole.

When you think about it, this is where the true potential of democracy lies. By growing and developing, citizens lay the groundwork for the overall development of society. Remember our discussion of self-authorship in

Parts I and II? As with organisations, any democratic society that aims to respect the needs of global humanity and the boundaries of the ecosystem relies on two things. First, it must provide parameters for the sustainable self-organisation of individuals and societies, aiming to re-embed humanity into the boundaries of the ecosystem. Second, it needs citizens who, by unfolding, developing and deepening their creative human abilities, expand their ability to take into account the well-being of the greater whole. The development of their consciousness is the prerequisite for them to not only take care of their personal well-being, but also the well-being of 'others' – other nations, other species, the planet as a whole.

Taking all these thoughts into account, we begin to see three parameters that define the contours of a new democratic purpose. We realise that any democratic purpose fit for the 21st and 22nd centuries must continue to include individual well-being, but must also transcend it as a sole focus.

> **First**, any democratic purpose fit for the future must encourage and further the reintegration of democratic societies within the boundaries of the ecosystem. This is a *sine qua non*: if democracy does not achieve this, it loses its legitimacy as a system that is supposed to enable society to create a good future.

> **Second**, and within the limits of the first parameter, democracy must create the conditions for a society that survives and thrives in the long term.

> **Third**, democracy must ensure a space for individual and collective development that transcends the sole focus on material well-being. In doing so, it provides citizens with the opportunity to develop their human qualities and potential. Thus, any democracy fit for the future must provide the infrastructure that facilitates and catalyses individual and collective development.

A democratic purpose that re-channels the creative energy of society towards ecological reintegration, making sure that the essential psychological, social, spiritual and material needs of its citizens are being met: this ideal is far from what we have today. Yet a clear, ambitious purpose like this can help to create a pull towards a future where democratic societies can exist and thrive in the long term. When we take this purpose seriously, we see that even democracy itself is just an instrument – used to create a space that enables the creation of a conscious, sustainable society. The mechanisms we choose for democracy to realise that purpose can be reimagined. Yes, there may be structures in today's society that are worth preserving. But there is also a need for new ones: new ground rules, new institutions, new processes that help to rebuild society in a meaningful way.

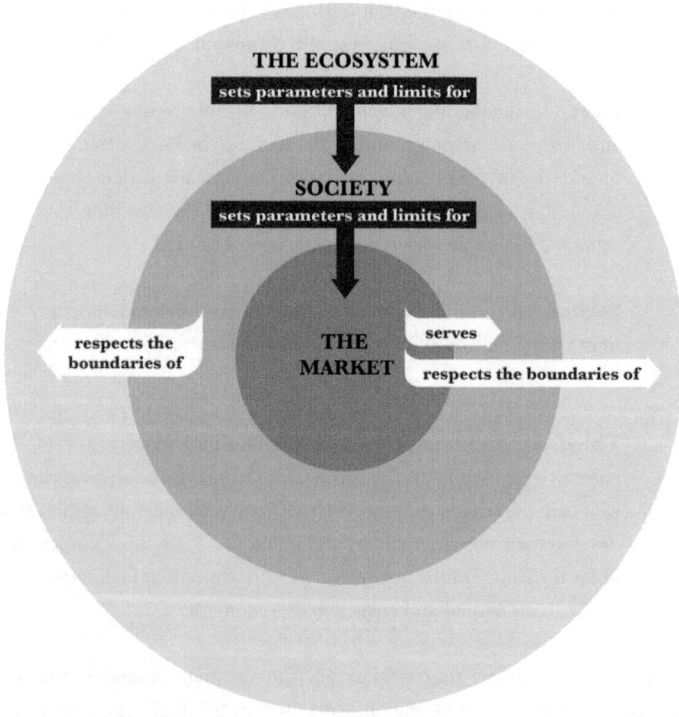

Figure 8 The Model We Need

Parameters of self-organisation: the dynamics that make transformation

The acknowledgement of the learned self and the definition of a purpose help to lay the foundation for societal transformation. In the next chapter, we will look at levers that help society take actual steps of transformation. Before we go there, let us take some time to understand the two basic dynamics that 'make' societal transformation. The first is self-organisation in society, the driving 'bottom-up' force that will bring the new to life. The second is radical reform: the political 'top-down' setting of parameters that steer and shape self-organisation according to the societal purpose.

Let us discuss societal self-organisation first. Over recent decades, modern democracy has developed – more intentionally than any other modern political system – the capability for individual and collective self-organisation. It emphasises the importance of individuals creating and designing their lives. It explicitly expects civil society to organise many aspects of social and collective interests. The subsidiary principle in the EU or states like Germany – which says that political and social issues should always be dealt with on the 'lowest' level possible – is a generalised invitation to participate within society. This makes liberal democratic systems different from autocratic systems, which aim for a higher degree of centralised control. While the latter systems fear too much self-organisation, democracies thrive on it.

When you think about it, modern democracy's strong emphasis on societal self-organisation is a key asset for successfully mastering the transformation needed in the decades to come. Self-organisation is what enables societal adaptation and innovation – two things we will need to see more of in the near future if Western societies want to conquer the profound challenges they face. Decentralised, self-organised collaboration is a vital resource for transformation. At the same time, we should not make the mistake of thinking self-organisation is a positive *per se*. The ambivalent results of today's self-organised market remind us of that. Whether societal self-organisation turns out to be a curse or blessing depends on the ground rules that shape and direct its forces within society. Self-organisation always mirrors the frame that steers and limits it – a frame that is designed politically. Only within this frame do individuals and society self-organise, as communities, as civil society, as scientists, as market innovators, as political forces…

Understanding this interdependent dynamic between politics and societal self-organisation is crucial. Indeed, the parameters politics and the state define – or the parameters they fail to define – *always* have systemic consequences for how society self-organises, whether citizens are aware of it or not. Think about where and how roads are built in a city. As physical limits they profoundly influence how people self-organise. People adapt the ways in which they use the streets according to where these roads are, and how they are designed: broad or narrow, green or grey, loud or silent, dangerous or safe. The city's inhabitants, mostly without noticing why they are doing what they do, react with specific patterns towards if, where and how streets are designed. It determines which way they walk to work, where they stroll for leisure, when and how they use cars and bicycles. This self-organised response is to some extent unintentional; the people adapt their behaviour automatically and without conscious deliberation. Yet the decision on how these roads are built was made intentionally. At some point, a person consciously designed the road layout, setting a frame that then steers unconscious behaviour, and thus defining a parameter for self-organisation. This action should not be mistaken for control of subsequent patterns. It is an impulse that then allows patterns of self-organised responses.

The way roads are built is just one of many examples. Indeed, societal self-organisation is influenced by a myriad of top-down parameters. There are explicit ones like the constitution or laws, and implicit ones like the unwritten norms and traditions of a society. At the level of national politics, a constitution accords certain values and norms an explicitly high status, and draws red lines for certain individual and political decisions. Social norms of how to behave in public steer how we interact with other people. Laws and regulations influence our behaviour in a broad range of contexts. All these parameters influence both individual and collective behaviour, enclosing the possible range of decision-making within certain boundaries. At the same time, they never *control* people's behaviour. In the end, it is up to our individual decision whether we adhere to a societal norm, whether we share the values of the constitution, or whether we respect regulations and laws. What these parameters ensure is that the basic defaults of collective behaviour are roughly aligned.

To put it differently, whenever you have a social system (with more than one human), there is an elementary need for different kinds of common parameters. Otherwise, living together as one society is, in the long term, impossible. It is critical to keep this in mind when we talk about societal transformation. We do not have to figure out what exactly a transformed society will look like – indeed it is certain that we cannot figure this out before the process of transformation begins. Self-organisation will produce the answers. What we must figure out, though, is which parameters we must establish – how we must re-design the societal frame – to orient individual and collective self-organisation into a meaningful direction that serves the purpose we sketched out above.

What follows from this task is the subsequent question: how do we put new, meaningful parameters into place? This, of course, is what politics and political reform are there for. In the late 1990s, Alberto Mangabeira Unger, an influential thinker on democracy, wrote about the *radical reforms* it takes to 'realise democracy'. He wrote that 'reform is radical when it addresses and changes the basic arrangements of a society; its formative structure of its institutions and enacted beliefs; it is reform because it deals with one discrete part of this structure at a time.' What differentiates radical reform from incremental reform, in other words, is that it concerns everyone in society; that it shapes the basic dynamics of self-organisation. It alters society's ground rules – step by step, with democratic means. This is the opposite of a revolutionary approach, which aims to transform everything at once. It is the realistic approach to how we transform society: with radical incrementalism.

The essential step towards realising a different reality is the creation of ideas for radical reform, and the organisation of political power to realise them. To achieve this, we must use the tools and levers democracy provides us with to set changes in motion that, sooner rather than later, will create a system that better meets the needs and challenges of humans and the planet we live on than today's democracy does. Politics, as we will discuss in the following chapter, is not the problem. It is a big part of the solution.

9 Accessing the Future

Levers for transforming society
(levers towards the new – iii)

IN THE previous two chapters, we sped through the multiple crises our society is in and developed an understanding of how important it is to find a new purpose for democratic society, a purpose that is focused on re-integrating us into the boundaries of the ecosystem while enabling its citizens to flourish. We discussed how societal self-organisation is the key resource for shaping the transformation that lies ahead. Lastly, we introduced the idea of radical reform, the transformation of societal parameters with democratic means.

In Part I of this book, we discussed the individual journey from learned self to core self. In Part II we saw how organisations can co-create a shared sense of purpose, and, by transforming in accordance with it, become prototypes for the transformation of greater social systems. As we saw, the transformation of individuals and organisations – while different in many ways – have parallel dynamics and intricate interdependencies. The one cannot work without the other.

The same is valid when we make the connection between societal transformation and the transformation of individuals and organisations. As we discussed, the transformation of the former is vastly more complex than the transformation of the latter. Yet, here as well, we can find parallel dynamics and strong interdependencies between all three dimensions.

To clarify this, let us translate the model of transformation we used in Parts I and II (see Figure 9): behind us lies our societal past – the known – with all its gains and pains, detours and disasters. It is a vast resource of experience. Some parts of it are useful for providing orientation for our way forward, while others hinder us from progressing towards a meaningful direction. Before us lies the future, or the unknown. Both 'external' and 'internal' factors push society towards leaving the status quo behind. Externally, the symptoms of the socio-ecological and the democratic crises show us that society must unlearn some of its destructive patterns it cultivated in the past. Internally, core knowledge lets every one of us feel a sense of spiritual unease: the deep humming of fear that brings us to understand that the 'external' crises amount, actually, to an internal one.

The combination of the status quo's discomfort and the fear of the unknown territory before us makes society feel paralysed; we know we must move, but we don't know where to or how. Yet there are certain factors that may potentially increase the societal sense of orientation and confidence: a purpose that fits the needs of today and tomorrow, or radical reform, to name two powerful pull factors.

In this chapter, we will discuss four levers that encourage societal unlearning, and thus the movement into the unknown: levers that help us initiate meaningful collective transformation by facilitating the imagination of realities beyond the current one; levers which, ultimately, are aimed at the rediscovery of our agency to unmake and transform the human-made world we live in.

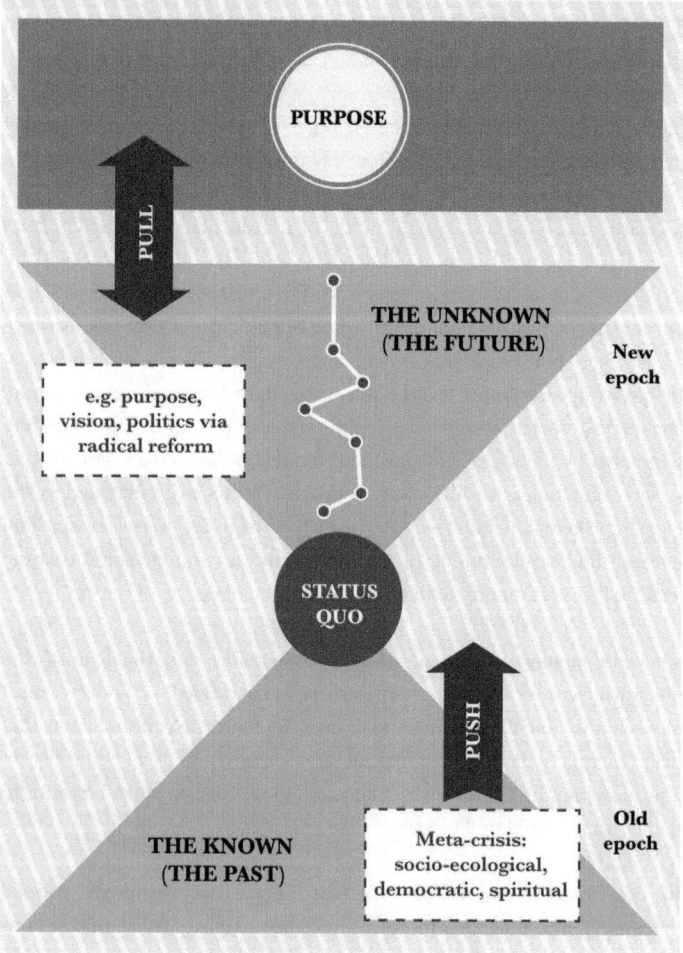

Figure 9 Societal Transformation

Lever 1: dismantling our belief in the permanence of the status quo

In the previous two chapters, we repeatedly touched upon how hard it is for us to imagine a different kind of society. This has roots in an underlying belief – the belief that it is impossible to transform our societies; that we are incapable of transcending the status quo, and taking successful steps towards a more meaningful direction. Such beliefs not only surround us they also paralyse us. When we don't believe in our capability to change the world we live in, we won't even bother to try. Accordingly, the first lever for transforming our societies is naming and tackling this underlying belief. Radical reform – substantial steps towards the creation of a different reality – is impossible if we harbour the idea that reality cannot be changed.

When you think about it, the widespread disbelief in our ability to change the world we live in is highly paradoxical. More than ever before in human history, we live in a reality that is almost exclusively defined by human-made constructs. Take our perspective on the economy as an example. When you think about it, it is nothing but a fictional entity made up of further fictional entities. Everything – its rules, its laws, its contracts, the very idea of money – are thin air once society decides to stop believing in them. At the same time, we are surrounded by the conviction that the market's rules cannot be changed. We created a system constituted entirely by the beliefs and actions of humans. It is a force of our own doing, a product of the amazing human ability to create things that are manifest only because we decide they should be so.

It is our belief that creates reality, and in this case our belief in a lack of alternatives to the status quo. If societal beliefs change, everything changes. If a critical number of people realised that there are other feasible ways to organise our economy, and thus the market that serves it, many of the everyday actions we today see as normal could be replaced by more sensible ones. The same is true of the states we live in. The police and military, parliaments and ministries, schools and city halls: what gives these institutions meaning is the societal belief in them. When we subtract this trust, nothing remains. Think of the collapse of the German Democratic Republic in 1989. The shared meaning that once was attributed to its institutions evaporated into thin air once a critical number of people ceased to believe that their state was able to care for their well-being, or that they must act in accordance with what state authorities wanted. They ceased to believe that the Wall was there to protect them, or that the secret police existed to serve the people. Their focus shifted. Instead of criticising singular rules and policies, they questioned the overall frame of their state.

Today's situation in Western democracies is different from the situation in the GDR in 1989. Yet we should ask ourselves what we can learn from examples like this one. After all, there is a parallel we should take very seriously: today's increasing withdrawal of societal trust from the political and economic system, hand in hand with the rising conviction that today's and tomorrow's challenges will not be solved by today's institutions. What we must ask ourselves is how we deal with this dynamic. Do we see it as an opportunity to productively consider meaningful alternatives to today's political and economic status quo? Or do we choose to leave the status quo untouched, as we helplessly watch the trust fundament of society erode? Depending on which option we choose, there are enormous consequences for the entire nature of societal discourse. We can continue to ignore the erosion and focus the public debate on incremental changes here and there. Or we can make use of the rising uncertainty to start a conversation on how the frame of politics and the economy can itself be rebuilt.

Think of it this way: imagine you are playing a board game. You and your friends are in the middle of a game, but nobody is really enjoying it. The question is: how fundamental is your discontent? Perhaps you like the game overall, but dislike some specific rules and design elements? Then it will suffice to intervene on a level that leaves the basic logic of the game untouched, just tweaking some of the more specific rules. But suppose you think the problems run deeper, to the core of the game structure. You're going to need some bigger changes. Maybe you take out a die, change the turn order, reduce or enlarge the number of players. We're now talking about interventions that change the fundamental dynamic of the game, a reconfiguration of its basic rules.

Our current political debates are tacitly but firmly structured around the intention to *not* discuss certain rules of the game. We have come to consider many of the human-made ground rules of our society and the global market to be permanent and unalterable, as much a given as the markings on a game board. We fervently discuss the minor rules of our game: details of the tax code, migration policy, pension rates. We've come to believe that such questions are what politics is about. We are so focused on adjusting details within the existing frame that we forget this frame is itself up for discussion! What we fail to talk about is which of today's political and economic parameters truly serve the deeper needs of today's and tomorrow's societies – and how we can reconfigure them if they don't.

As long as the fundamental, human-made rules of the world around us remain a blind spot, as long as we believe in *this* reality's unalterable state, it will remain an eternal monolith. If we, on the other hand, decide to unlearn this belief, we can create a moment where the supposedly eternal shows its fluid and alterable face.

This is what radical reform is for: to change the alterable, to transform the supposedly permanent. In fact, our history is strewn with powerful examples that remind us of the impermanence of supposedly unalterable realities. The abolition of slavery. The abolition of child labour. The implementation of social security systems. Women's suffrage. The creation of the European Union. All these radical reforms had fundamental impacts on the whole of society – and all of them were preceded by the general and firmly held belief that such reforms were politically impossible, as they ran counter to learned patterns that seemed perfectly normal. Think about it: the economy of the young United States fundamentally relied on slavery. In early modern capitalism, child labour was assumed an absolute necessity. Social security systems for the working class seemed like a utopian dream throughout the early decades of the 19th century. Women's suffrage ran counter to the centuries-old belief that women neither deserve nor desire the right to political self-determination. The creation of the United Nations and the European Union followed the ideological conviction that nations cannot and should not cooperate. Yet radical reforms, realised through the democratic process, fundamentally changed these societal realities – an expression of the collective realisation that things must not stay as they are: that reality, indeed, can be changed.

Why would the societies of the 19th and 20th centuries be able to implement radical reform – and us not? Why would we believe that transformation is impossible if we know it has successfully been done in the past? What these historic examples remind us of is that transformation is not a simple, external act. Transformation, first and essentially means the transformation of our belief systems; it means the inner process of rethinking and reimagining. Imagining the transformation is a prerequisite to implementing it.

Lever 2: ideating radical reforms

Just as we can reflect on and change beliefs, we can change the rules that are based on these beliefs. Transformation may seem like a big thing. But in complex systems, even relatively small interventions can create transformative dynamics that change the system as a whole. This is where radical reform comes in; reforms that have the potential to spark the positive transformation of society as a whole.

For a long time now, we have lived in a world that lacked transformational political ideas due to its belief that the fundamentals of our systems are not up for discussion. Public discourse focused on incremental reform, small changes that left the parameters of our system untouched. Only in recent years have more radical ideas for reform gained popularity, ideas like the universal basic income, for instance, or the creation of a European Republic would change the basic dynamics of how our societies work and affect every citizen: radical reforms in the purest sense.

Yet the number of ideas for radical reform we publicly discuss remains extremely limited. I believe that this lack of transformative reform proposals is caused by a common misperception: that political parties, elected politicians and experts are the ones to come up with ideas for reform. This, of course, is a very flawed notion once we consider the actual functions and strengths of these groups. Political parties and politicians are the ones whose job it is to convert ideas into laws, and to broker political compromise. Experts are tasked with finding ways to implement ideas that have public support. But *ideating* them – that is a task for civil society. It is something *we* must do, faster and more numerous than we have done at any time in recent decades.

If we create a situation where more and more radical reform ideas become part of public discourse, politics will be under increasing pressure to implement them. Radical reform will happen when radical ideas are the new normal – not while we treat these ideas as the exception.

Yet the question remains: how can we come up with more and better ideas for radical reform? A central lever lies in the societal conversations about the future we desire, our purpose and our values. These conversations enable us to derive specific ideas: radical reforms we must realise in alignment with our vision, purpose and values.

As we discussed in the last chapter, today's Western societies chronically lack a sense of purpose. Yet we can still make use of universally accepted values like 'peace', 'justice' or 'equality', embedded in many of the constitutions of Western democracies, as access points for conversations that lead us towards the ideation of radical reforms. One way to do this is to ask citizens how they would describe a future where the values society promotes today are fully realised. This results in fragments of a positive vision – a vision that strategically enables us to design steps that society must take now to develop towards it.

To give a quick example, let us return to the value of liberty. As we saw in Chapter 7, today's societies are built on the belief that producing and consuming whatever we want is an inherent part of the democratic freedom we enjoy. While we all suffer the consequences of this extremist notion, a small number of corporations massively profit from it.

Let us imagine, as a nutshell example, a society where a different understanding of liberty is realised – a liberty that takes into account the well-being of the greater systems human civilisation is part of. A society that sees sustainability as the inevitable flipside of prosperity, knowing that liberty in the long-term can only be guaranteed if human society is an integral, regenerative part of the ecosystem. This society deems economic activity that significantly reduces the liberty of other people, species or generations illegitimate. The state actively enables its citizens to live carbon-neutral, by enacting ground rules and regulations that prevent the externalisation of negative costs.

What follows is a change of perspective. Which steps would we, as members of this future society, urge today's society to take towards this positive vision? Which systemic, radical reforms would we urge today's political decision-makers to realise? Considering our future society's self-understanding as a regenerative part of the ecosystem, one potential reform that comes to mind is this: profit that is made with stocks heavily reliant on cost-externalisation is taxed more heavily than profit from other stocks. Whoever holds shares in a company that significantly harms the environment and public health with its actions has to pay an Externalisation Compensation Tax on dividends. Besides disincentivising investment in these companies, this would also mean that revenues of cost-externalising companies flow not to shareholders but into public funds, where they can be used for measures that benefit society and the ecosystem. This reform would alter the logic of investing, and thus entire market dynamics. Suddenly, every investor would be forced to take into consideration the environmental and social consequences a business model has, instead of focusing exclusively on its profit margins, as is the case today. At the same time, these changes would equate to a massive incentivisation of sustainable business models and the acceleration of existing businesses' ecological transformation.

This is but one example. I am sure you could come up with another, better idea – which is exactly my point. Ideating radical reforms is something we can and should be undertaking as a civil society. It is not to be outsourced to political parties or ministries. These players are too tightly entangled in the limited perspectives of their everyday realities. Instead of dreaming of a better world, they will tell you why such a world can never be realised, and which forces and regulations will hinder you from realising the reforms you may come up with… The ideation of radical reform is thus something you and I and everyone must do. The more attractive our vision, the more specific our ideas and the more compelling the stories by which we deliver them, the more likely it is that more and more people realise: *it doesn't have to be the way it is now.*

Lever 3: rediscovering (party) politics

If you're a politically experienced person reading this, no doubt at this moment you have many arguments in your head, about how everything is actually a lot more complicated than the picture I've painted over the last few pages. You may be thinking of well-organised class and economic interests that make most radical reforms impossible. Maybe you're thinking of the immense difficulty involved in coordinating such measures with other national governments. You may say that most parts of society are afraid of more fundamental changes. You may say how hard it is to argue for radical reform in media cycles that work with 15-second soundbites. All true! Things are complex, and transformative steps are no easy thing to achieve. At the same time, all these reasons mostly serve as excuses to do nothing, to accept reality as it is. It is so easy to focus with all our energy on why something we theoretically find right will *not* work in practice. We have become the master explainers for our own lack of agency. Isn't that what we should be worried about? That we don't even try?

I believe we must dare to try, more boldly than we have over the past decades. After all, coming up with a vision for society and ideating radical reforms is only the beginning. To *implement* such transformative steps takes people who argue and fight for them, who organise a majority of votes, and who make sure these transformative measures are realised properly. In other words, it takes what it takes to get things done politically. I know this sounds terribly un-sexy to some ears. This pragmatic aspect of societal transformation is something which many people disdain. Their general dislike of establishment politics has created a blind spot for the productive function of politics as part of any successful transformation process.

I've had countless conversations with activists who told me how they avoid engaging directly with political apparatus and decision-makers. Too frustrating, they say. Too arduous. Too depressing. They prefer to trust the bottom-up dynamics of civil society to change things and hope that transformation will emerge by itself. Well, what a mistake! Yes, transformation needs bottom-up dynamics. But whoever aims to implement transformative reforms on a societal level must understand that without political power and the right people in executive and legislative institutions, radical reform will be impossible. Top-down decision-making in political institutions must be part of any serious transformative game plan. This requires the organisation of political power, and thus building alliances that go beyond the like-minded few. Only these things combined offer a chance to achieve meaningful transformative steps via the democratic process.

What is currently missing are new political players who bundle transformative reform ideas, the ability to unite and mobilise, and the political power and know-how to translate ideas into written law. Getting there may be easier than it sounds. The current political landscape is so uninspired and weak that a fairly small, well-coordinated group of people with a clear, shared purpose, and shared ideas for radical reform could quickly gain substantial political and discursive power. This is something we can learn from the last decade's political rise of neo-nationalist forces all over the Western world. What made them so successful is that they managed better than others to combine a shared intent with an ability to organise politically. They found people with a shared ideological agenda, who organised their friends and neighbours. They found people who funded them. They were willing to spend time and energy on the political game.

This sounds trivial, and indeed it is. The current neo-nationalist political successes all around the Western world are made possible by the weakness of established political parties and an immobilised civil society. For many years now, centrist parties have failed to organise meaningful societal conversations: what kind of society we aim to be (purpose), how we can tangibly enact societal values (values), and which steps we must take to make things better (radical reform). Established political parties are out of touch with the future – they navigate the status quo, absorbed in debates on how to change the ornaments of today's game. This leaves space for political actors who are willing to do things differently; who understand that incrementalism has ceased to be the right modus operandi, and who are willing to tap into the transformative potential of the political process.

Luckily, parallel to the rise of the nationalist right, new political parties and movements have been founded all over the Western world: organisations like Alternativet in Denmark, municipalist movements like Barcelona en

Comù in Spain, or Razem in Poland. What unites these new players is that their work is based on different paradigms from those of established parties. They focus on system transformation. And most of them experiment with structural elements of the self-authoring organisation, as discussed in Chapter 5. Their organisations thus work differently from established political parties. They are based on a clear purpose and values, which, in some cases, are results of co-creation. Decision-making authority is decentralised, while a culture of collaboration is promoted, especially by enabling people to co-create and contribute online.

These new parties may not be ready to take the place of bigger, established ones yet. But they are alive and kicking, and will almost certainly be joined by additional new parties over the coming years. Which is to say: yes, centrist, established parties may be dying. But we should not confuse their death with the death of the political party *per se*. Actually, it would be a huge mistake to turn our backs on this concept at this moment in history. As far as I can see, political parties are the only organisations that have the potential to bring together ideas, intent and the realisation of meaningful reforms via the organisation of political power.

But it takes a collective effort to build parties that give life to this role: parties that understand themselves as institutions which organise society-wide dialogues on our shared future; parties that bring people together who usually do *not* talk to each other; parties that take responsibility for spelling out the results of this dialogue into laws and regulations; transformative forces that refocus the political landscape towards decisions that matter.

Any new party that wants to create significant impact must build its actions upon two insights. First, the goal must be to shift the strategic axes of the political playing field. Any tactical positioning upon today's spectrum between the incrementalist left and right will lead to failure. What is needed is the positioning as a transformative force, in contrast to the incrementalist forces of the political establishment. To go back to the above analogy of the board game, the key lies in altering the ground rules of the game. This means shifting the focus of the political discourse, away from changing the details of the existing picture towards reconfiguring its frame.

Second, any transformative force must come up with new formats that redefine how the political conversation is organised. We have already discussed the need to focus the public conversation on purpose, values and vision. Currently, we lack formats and spaces for such societal dialogue, spaces which help shift perspective, help to create a joined-up vision, and which inquire into what it takes to get there. David Bohm, a physicist and philosopher, wrote about how dialogue must mean a lot more than 'conversation' to bring about new insights. Bohm wrote about 'the ability to hold many points of view in suspension, along with a primary interest in the creation of common meaning'. It is this 'common meaning' that is central. Nothing less is required for societies to leave their current state of paralysis.

David Bohm developed a setting which pushes participants towards a radically different attitude from the ones we are used to. To name some principles: the conversation must be without pre-defined output. The focus lies on listening, instead of focusing on what you have to say. The dialogue offers no space for debate, placing the focus on collaboratively evolving new perspectives and insights. The fascinating thing about this setting is that it creates an open space for new insights and ideas. By suspending your own opinion, by attempting to empty your mind in order to better listen to other people's point of view, and by intentionally slowing down the conversation, space for the emergence of a shared new perspective is created.

Being simply a format, dialogue will not solve the challenges we face. But it can be a fundament for new political parties to come up with perspectives that bear the potential for deeper societal transformation. It lays the groundwork for a societal climate that is able to productively hold difference, and to think from a shared perspective instead of a divisive one. The challenge for a transformative political party thus lies in creating and scaling up spaces where such dialogue can be practised. If such a party manages to do so, something new will become possible: new experiences, new perspectives, new ideas.

Lever 4: spiritualising the public conversation

To expand and deepen the public conversation, we must not only build new spaces and formats. We must also shift the inner place from which we speak. This is where we, as individuals, can make a significant difference. Do we speak about the course of society solely from a place of rational thought and judgement? Or do we include the subtle dimensions of ourselves into how and what we articulate in conversation with others? Do we solely speak about what we are sure of, or do we include what we fear, and where we feel lost when we consider our common future?

In Parts I and II, we discussed how, as individuals and organisations, we can only change our patterns if we develop a clear sight of our learned self, in order to then unlearn the patterns that hinder us from moving forward. This requires, as a first vital step, an honest look into the mirror, and the acceptance of what is there. Only then can we start identifying the patterns that keep us from moving forward, and to unlearn what we learned to see as normal. I am convinced that, as an overall dynamic, this is required for society as well. This process must happen not individually, but in dialogue that transcends the boundaries of our everyday lives. We will only be able to transform as society if we manage to collectively face the degree to which we have learned to distort our collective self-image. As society, the acceptance of our learned self is the precondition for transforming it.

The entry point for developing the collective competence of unlearning is acknowledging and embracing the collective fear we share. As we considered in Chapter 7, there is an intensifying, underlying sense of fear and shame that transcends the societal boundaries of lifestyles, milieus, political parties, generations and faiths. A collective inkling that we may be on the wrong side of history. Despite all our auto-suggestive stories about our supreme democracies, our high recycling quota and our energy-efficient cars, we slowly realise that we are destroying the world as we know it, existentially threatening billions who are not to blame for the ecological and spiritual mess we are in. Acknowledging these feelings, and thus naming the terror we exercise upon this world, can bring a significant unburdening. It enables us to refocus: from constantly window-dressing a broken home to building a new one.

Accessing this collective state can be done by starting a conversation on its symptoms. The epidemic of mental suffering and illness, for instance, is affecting every one of us. We all have touchpoints with it, be it our own story of suffering, or through the experience of seeing suffering people around us. A general feeling of unease and unhappiness is omnipresent. People comprehend that this mushrooming depression cannot exclusively be attributed to individual psychological crises. This crisis around us is a crisis *within* us. What we experience as individual suffering mirrors a suffering of society which, while we may treat the symptoms at the level of the individual, can only be cured at the systemic level of the cause.

When you start conversations about such a topic, people usually quickly bring up the systemic nature of such problems. The conversation's focus quickly expands towards thoughts about the way of life we have chosen, and how people feel both lured by and trapped in it. People understand that their individual behaviour is a fractal of a collective state. They realise that the focus on individual suffering and healing may not suffice if millions or even billions share the same state of unease one feels as a single human being. They long for relief.

In other words, there are inklings of core knowledge everywhere – a spiritual inkling that tells us from deep within ourselves that we must collectively change course; that we must unlearn. It is behind this inkling where we will discover transformational solutions of shared acceptance.

Acknowledging these silent needs and desires, implicit knowledge, spiritual inklings – this has been afforded no space in our public conversation, at least, not since the dawn of modernity. After many decades of secularised, rational discourse, we have pushed such parts of human life into the private space, and religious and spiritual niche discourse. This also is something we must unlearn, and we must accept that our fears, desires and hopes deserve to be talked about. They contain relevant information for our future.

Yet spiritualising public discourse requires an individual willingness to break with learned patterns of how we speak in public. To pose open questions, instead of providing people with answers. In the professional political space, this is a radical departure from what is familiar in the status quo, which tends to sneer at people who venture beyond the impersonal and rationalised. At the same time, there are many others who react with curiosity, trust and gratitude when someone is able to expand the limits of the speakable.

So maybe – just maybe – having a few spiritualised people in the political arena could be the first spark for building a new transformative alliance. One that counts on vulnerability and love, not strength and distrust. One that stresses our shared destiny, not competition. One that builds on the potential of emergence instead of relying on the boundaries of the status quo. When we begin this work, we start a process of collective healing, which takes the humming of fear as the starting point, progresses by acknowledging the dissonance that distorts our lives and actions, and continues by searching for inklings of the new. This is a healing that reaches the realisation: yes, we can be different. Yes, reality is impermanent. Yes, transformation is possible.

Epilogue

AFTER READING this book you may think: we have a long, rocky way ahead of us. Society, almost every organisation I know, and certainly many of us individually are torn between the desire to avoid the discomforts of transformation, and the cognitive insight that leaving things as they are is not an option. The unknown lies right ahead of us, and for most of us it is a very scary territory to enter. This is why we invest all our energy in stabilising the status quo, hoping to be able to postpone a journey towards something different.

In one moment in history, an unexpected shock made us realise that transformation may happen faster than most of us believe to be possible. The Covid-19 pandemic reminded us of our ability to fundamentally change course, at least for a while. For a short moment, we grasped that, indeed, things could be fundamentally different if we really wanted to see them transformed. In the early stages of the Covid-19 crisis, it seemed like, suddenly, the We was more important than the I. Individuals changed their life from one day to the next, just as many organisations overthrew their modus operandi. On the political level, the autopilot of incrementalism was stopped. The primacy of the economic was put on hold, clearly trumped by the primacy of the political. Radical reforms were discussed and, in a few cases, politicians successfully pushed for renegotiating the frame.

At the same time, and as an extra push towards transformation, the pandemic brought to the surface how fragile and unjust our systems are. As so often, the poorest and weakest suffered the most, with the working class a lot less shielded than the more privileged parts of society. In many countries, the public health systems proved to be porose, incapable of dealing with this moment's demands due to years of severe austerity. Democratically elected politicians in England, the US, Brazil and other countries did everything to keep the economic wheel spinning, which benefited mostly the super-rich while sacrificing thousands who died of the virus. As a consequence, the crisis propelled a process of societal self-reflection: what kind of society are we, really? Are we as just, as inclusive, as we like to believe? Is there really no alternative to an economic system so vulnerable and unjust? The crisis turned out to be a short, precious moment of collective introspection. It led broad parts of society towards acknowledging a more nuanced picture of the societies we have become.

It was interesting to see how, in this moment, there seemed to be an opening for new, unconventional ideas for radical reform and societal transformation. It seemed like both politics and mainstream society were more willing to take in new perspectives, and actually reflect on their viability. At the same time, during this opening, we painfully realised how much we lack both purpose and vision that would have enabled Western societies to more forcefully foster transformation, and to use the momentum the pandemic provided us with.

In the coming years, we will be confronted more and more often with shock events like the Covid-19 pandemic. The fallout of the climate crisis, and the increasing geopolitical fragility will force us to deal with structural shock events whose exact nature is impossible to predict today. This brings with it the necessity to do everything we can to increase societal resilience, while decreasing the factors which, as of today, catalyse the very crises we will be dealing with in the near future. On the political level, this means focusing on rebuilding the societal frame to make it more fit for the future than it is today. We are in urgent need of activists and politicians who are willing to understand themselves as transformative forces who shift the debate from the incremental to the fundamental, who are willing to reinvent political parties, and to rebuild democratic institutions via radical reform, in a way fit for the second half of the 21st century.

In reaction to our shifting societal environments, we will be witnessing a fundamental shift in the organisational world as well. Those who decide to be drivers of transformation, and who understand themselves as both servants and fractals of overall society, have exciting decades of development ahead of them. Their challenge lies in building organisations that are both resilient and highly adaptive. If these experimental spaces manage to cultivate self-authorship, and to establish functional self-organisation, the whole of society will benefit massively.

Individually, the increasing instability of our environments carries the responsibility of finding stability in ourselves. Personal transformation – the journey towards our core, and the alignment of our learned self with core knowledge, our purpose and values – is the first step towards meaningfully transforming the communities we are part of. If we manage to become someone else individually, our communities and society as a whole will too, sooner or later. This, of course, is not a call for atomised individual introspection. Today's challenge – for all of us – lies in walking the path of individual transformation without becoming entirely absorbed by that journey. After all, this journey is not mainly about ourselves, but about what we can cultivate and contribute to further the greater whole.

This idea equals a great responsibility: to take the focus and time we need to explore and transform ourselves, to expand our individual depth and energy. But, in order to unleash our transformative power, and to have an effect on the greater systems we are part of, we must walk this path in close relation with others. We must share both our pain and insights so that those around us can (un-)learn. Doing so helps us to not regress to the known, and to spread the sense of purpose and direction we uncover along the way.

This, I believe, is the challenge we face. To be visible and touchable as beings of transformation, both vulnerable and powerful, doubtful yet purposeful. To understand our individual story as a story of what it means to be and develop as human being. By showing how we are becoming and unbecoming, we inspire those around us to explore their own paths of transformation. This is the fundament for the realisation of a transformed society: more integrated, more free, more like the selves we could be.

Epilogue

Acknowledgements

THIS BOOK will open new doors, and it will close some that are now open. Writing *Unlearn* was a bittersweet experience. It was bitter, as the logistical and intellectual boundaries of my everyday life limited the time and bandwidth for this project. The longer I wrote, the more I realised how much more substance I would have liked to consolidate, whether it be reading theory, talking to other thinkers and doers, or just by reflecting on the scope of this book on a deeper level. At the same time, it was a very sweet experience to sit down and do this. The time I took for writing this book enabled me to better understand myself, and to find coherent words where, before, I only had vague clusters of ideas.

In the course of writing this book, my life changed profoundly. I married, moved several times, founded and repeatedly reconfigured my company, godfathered several projects at the think tank Das Progressive Zentrum, facilitated an endless number of workshops, gave keynotes all over Europe, and wrote another book on transformative political parties. In retrospect, it is quite a miracle that I continued with this project despite all this – a miracle made possible by the generous support I received during the course of writing this book:

Unlearn would have remained unfinished without the great passion and focus that my London-based editor Rich Mason contributed. You pushed me when I was about to give up, and you made the text sharper and better than it would have been without your support.

Jonathan Rowson and Caspar Henderson of Perspectiva Press gave me a decisive nudge towards drastically cutting the length of the original manuscript, which made this book crisper. Ivo Juriaan Mensch and Jeremy Johnson took this project into their hands and drove it towards publishing. Johanna Robinson did the book a great service by giving it a very thorough proofread, and I am grateful to Alison Shakspeare for her professionalism in typesetting and design. My sister Catharina Burmester greatly supported me by translating my scribbles into professional illustrations.

Tomas Björkman's *The World We Create* inspired and influenced me and this book. Tomas was so kind to read an earlier, way messier version of this manuscript in early 2020. Thank you, Tomas, for your thoughts, your positive energy and the encouragement to consider Perspectiva Press.

Andreas Burmester, my father, helped me to realise decisive insights regarding my past when he re-opened the story of his great-aunt Ursula Murawski. Shortly before wrapping up this manuscript, he finished his book *Versandung*, a semi-fictional account of Ursula's life and death in the German psychiatric system of the 1930s (published in German by Vergangenheits-Verlag). The effort he put into the research, and the sharing of his materials with me, enabled me to include Ursula's story in Chapter 2. Also, my father kept asking about the book over the past few years, always trusting that I would finish it.

My work at the Democracy Lab of Das Progressive Zentrum enabled me to devote time and thinking to topics around the transformation of democracy and society. Chapters 7 and 8 are, in parts, based on my paper *Beyond (this) democracy*, which was published at the 2018 Innocracy Conference in Berlin. Parts of the Introduction are based on the keynote *A Challenge of Unbecoming* I held at the Innocracy Conference 2019.

The models in Chapter 7 are inspired by talks and presentations by both Maja Göpel and Lance Bennett at the 2017 Innocracy Conference in Berlin.

Jan Eriksson and Dominic von Martens graciously and warm-heartedly shared Self Leaders' approach to values work in organisations, which is mirrored in Chapters 3 and 6. I deeply value the trust you put in my young company a couple of years ago.

And then there were those who did something essential: permanent nudging.

My husband Roma patiently endured the ups and downs of the writing process, gently pushing me towards continuing and finishing this project.

Christian Kaspar Schwarm constantly asked about this project, and kindly yet forcefully pushed me towards continuing to write. Your feedback on the abstract's first and last draft encouraged me not to compromise. You were one of the voices who supported the broad scope of this book from the start, which was really important.

Maximilian Benz read the cut manuscript in April 2020 and gave extremely helpful and generous comments. In 2018, while editing the text of his habilitation, he read the raw version of Chapter 7 in a deckchair in Sochi – I was very relieved you did not tear the text to pieces. Also, Max commented on my paper *Beyond (this) democracy*, which is the basis for Chapters 7 and 8.

Patrizia Nanz read my abstract and two of the book's chapters in late 2019 – her comments and support motivated me to continue with the manuscript.

Michaela Gilg graciously hosted two of my book retreats in her beautiful Bavarian sinecure. The grounded energy of your place and yours and your family's warm, welcoming energy helped me push this manuscript towards its finalisation.

Klara Sucher encouraged me to continue working on the manuscript in the early stages of writing this book.

After writing a rough draft of Part I, I hosted a book night for a few friends and colleagues. The support I received during that night motivated me to continue with this project. Thanks to Roma, Jone Szmania, Ben Mason, Philip Sälhoff, Michael Katzmann, Ilana Wetzler, Niclas Hille and all others who were there.

Jonathan Klodt encouraged me to write this book during a coaching session we had years ago, thus initiating a years-long creative process.

Steffen Stäuber put me in touch with Tomas Björkman and the Emerge network when he invited me into the cocreation.loft a couple of years ago. Thanks for this, Steffen.

While I decided to write neither a theoretical nor an academic book, I would still like to name a couple of books that influenced this text:

> Tomas Björkman, *The World We Create*, 2019
>
> Frijtof Capra/Pier Luigi Luisi, *The Systems View of Life*, 2014
>
> Lizabeth Cohen, *A Consumer's Republic*, 2003
>
> André Gorz, *Abschied vom Proletariat*, 1980
>
> Amitav Gosh, *The Great Derangement*, 2017
>
> Hermann Haken/Günther Schiepek, *Synergetik in der Psychologie*, 2010

Robert Kegan, *The Evolving Self*, 1983

Robert Kegan, *In Over Our Heads*, 1995

Naomi Klein, *This Changes Everything*, 2015

Frédéric Laloux, *Reinventing Organisations*, 2013

Jonathan Rowson, *Spiritualise*, 2014

Otto Scharmer, *Theory U*, 2007

Roberto Unger, *Democracy Realized*, 2000

If you are interested in reading more about the positive potential of transformative political parties, something I only lightly touched upon in Chapter 9, check out Clemens Holtmann's and my book *Liebeserklärung an eine Partei, die es nicht gibt*, published by Quadriga Verlag in March 2021.

Finally, I want to thank you for reading this book. Please recommend it to others if you liked it.

Hanno Burmester, December 2020